What people are saying about DRIVING LESSONS and Jim R. Jacobs

"*Driving Lessons* is full of inspiring, humorous, and thought-provoking stories that will absolutely change your life!"

— Barbara Murray, MSW, LCSW,
Author of *Taking Back Parenting*

"I have had the wonderful opportunity to hear and participate in presentations by Jim R. Jacobs. These have been extremely engaging, entertaining, and useful. He is able to involve an audience quickly and have people participate and learn throughout. He is masterful."

— Mark Tandberg, MSW, Church Leader,
Brighton, Colorado

"*Driving Lessons* is a fun ride! It is wonderful to receive great reminders to help you to become a better you and live better. If you want to get further down the road of life and be full of joy doing it, pick up a copy today."

— Brett Dupree, Author of *Joyous Expansion:
Unleashing Your Passions to Lead an Inspired Life*

"Jim Jacobs is a talented behavioral scientist and therapist who has the incredible ability to distill theory and thought into practical application"

— James T. Skeen, MS, LPC, Community Counselor,
Loveland, Colorado

"Let Jim R. Jacobs be your personal driving instructor. He knows how to take you down the road of life and help you to find more joy, more happiness, and more success."

— Carol Paul, Author of *Team Clean:*
The Ultimate Family Clean-Up-The-House Formula

"In this world of road rage, all of us can use some *Driving Lessons*. Jim reminds us of what is important in life, and artfully inspires us to change."

— James K Lehman, CPA, SPHR, Author of *Maneuvering Your*
Career: Taking Charge of Your Future, Owning Your Job,
and Achieving Your Dreams

"I've listened in wonder to Jim Jacobs teach. He is informed, energetic, and engaging. His counsel has produced results in the lives of those who've followed it. I hope he writes a dozen more books like this one."

— Mark McConkie, PhD, Church Leader

"Jim Jacobs masterfully draws parallels between daily driving and life's challenges as he relates his varied experiences and sage advice in his book *Driving Lessons*. Great lessons for everyone in any situation."

— Dr. Levi Murray, Author of *Succeeding by Choice*

"As a licensed marriage and family therapist, I am pleased to recommend Jim R. Jacobs as an awesome speaker and author. His topics and presentations are always inspiring to individuals, couples, and families!"

— Cameron R. Lorenc, MA, LMFT, Author of *Change Your*
Mind—Change Your Life! 44 Keys to a Happier, Healthier Family

"*Driving Lessons* will drive home important life lessons that will help you stay on the road to success."

— HC Joe Raymond, Author of
Embracing Change From the Inside Out

"Jim Jacobs' passion for teaching others is evident in the way he instructs. He produces personal growth and a desire to improve. I have been blessed with the opportunity to learn and grow from Jim's compassion and knowledge, and this will always be with me."

— Michael Oliver, LCSW, Chicago, Illinois

"In this world of high speeds, traffic jams, and rush hours, *Driving Lessons* is a breath of fresh air. Jim offers fun and refreshing stories to help you better live your life, find your truth, and be happier."

— Nicole Gabriel, Author of
Finding Your Inner Truth
Discovering Peace When Everything Changes

"Jim is not only an engaging speaker but a thoughtful and thought-provoking one as well. He is sensitive to the needs of the group and is always well prepared so he may present information that is useful, meaningful, and applicable to daily life."

— Melissa Aschenbrenner, LCSW,
Be of Good Cheer Services, Brighton, Colorado

"*Jim Jacobs* is a dedicated, experienced mental health professional with an engaging presentation style."

— Margaret Clark Zappitello, Ed.D., LPC, LAC,
Brighton, Colorado

"*Driving Lessons* teaches what you need to know to navigate better all the roads of life. It is perfect for the coffee table, the toilet, listening to on your commute or bus ride, or giving as gifts to others. Get ready for an exciting drive!"

— Patrick Snow, International Best-Selling Author of *Creating Your Own Destiny* and *The Affluent Entrepreneur*

"Jim Jacobs is a talented, wise, intuitive, intelligent, empowering, effective instructor. He leads by example, and he practices what he teaches."

— Michelle C. Evans, LCSW, Life Balance Revolution, Sacramento, California

"Anyone facing challenges in life will find him- or herself touched and uplifted by the insights and wisdom Jim Jacobs shares in this book! His candid and direct style combined with both humor and compassion are a refreshing mix!"

— Emily Macfarlane, MA, CLIMB Consultation Services, Mountain View, California

"Listening to Jim teach or present is always an engaging, insightful, and educational experience. He has a gift for bringing to light complex and real life topics in a manner that is easily relatable and personable. I leave his presentations filled spiritually, mentally, and emotionally. I discover such an abundance of information that I find myself returning to the ideas and imagery he offers, to ponder upon, repeatedly. Come prepared to capture priceless pearls of wisdom from Jim's insights and experiences, as you would from a heart-to-heart conversation with a good friend."

— Caralee Frederic, LCSW, CGT, Colorado Springs, Colorado

"Jim R. Jacobs takes a no nonsense approach to various topics he presents. He is compelling and intriguing and inspires those who listen and hear his message to apply his knowledge."

— Douglas R. Clawson, LCSW, Morrison, Colorado

"*Driving Lessons* is not your typical self-help/change book. Jim Jacobs takes the everyday experience you have behind the wheel of your car and turns it into compelling life lessons. After reading this memorable book, you'll have a new outlook on life each time you get on the road. Driving in your car will never feel the same."

— Debra A. Jason, MA, Author of
Millionaire Marketing on a Shoestring Budget

"Over the past few years, it has been my pleasure to know Jim R. Jacobs. He has been a speaker at workshops and firesides while I have served as a church leader. He is a wonderful speaker with the ability to keep a group engaged. I recommend him to any group who is looking for a dynamic presenter."

— James Jackson, Church Leader, Lakewood, Colorado

"If you ever read the book *Man of Steel and Velvet,* you will understand why Jim Jacobs epitomizes its concept. He is gentle, kind, and strong. His knowledge of people and how to deal with life is what makes him so successful. I enjoy my conversations with Jim and learn a great deal from him. I know that you will benefit greatly from reading this book."

— Denise Cleverley, Westminster, Colorado

"Jim R. Jacobs is a wonderful speaker with insights that allow us to apply his counsel to better our everyday lives."

— Alan J. Toth, Denver, Colorado

"Jim Jacobs has amazingly fresh insight. The stories and analogies in *Driving Lessons* are spot-on and memorable. His sensitivity and caring demeanor shine through in all his writings. He's a sharp, witty, and relevant teacher who will have you hanging on every word."

— Erin McClellan, *Cross Roads Journal*, Saratoga Springs, Utah

"Jim R. Jacobs has taught me things that will always stay with me and help me every day of my life. He has an amazing, healthy way of reframing trials and challenges and pain."

— Tracy Barrand, MA LPC, Evergreen Colorado

"Jim is an INSPIRATION! He continues to make an impact on the lives he touches every day. He has a special gift to INSPIRE and EMPOWER people and audiences to live their lives with more purpose and more passion."

— Teri Karjala, LPC, LMFT, Greenwood Village, Colorado

"*Driving Lessons For Life* dispenses concrete, practical advice on how to make the most of your life in a fun and refreshing way. As an added bonus to revisiting familiar concepts, you may well improve your driving skills."

— Susan Friedmann, CSP, international best-selling author of *Riches in Niches: How to Make it BIG in a small Market*

"Jim Jacobs combines insight with skill, helping individuals and families overcome their roadblocks and reach their potentials."

— Paul Sigafus, LMFT, Colorado Counseling Center,
Centennial, Colorado

"Jim R. Jacobs is a thoroughly delightful presenter. He manages to present in a clear manner that keeps you entertained while delivering well-researched and useful information. Jim's use of humor and metaphor helps bring his presentations alive for the audience in a meaningful and memorable fashion. I have always been totally engaged whenever I attend one of his presentations."

— Robert N. Turner, LPC, Littleton, Colorado

A FUN AND REFRESHING RIDE TO BETTER LIVING

DRIVING LESSONS

FOR LIFE

THOUGHTS ON
NAVIGATING YOUR ROAD
TO PERSONAL GROWTH

JIM R. JACOBS, LCSW

AVIVA
PUBLISHING
New York

Driving Lessons for Life
Thoughts on Navigating Your Road to Personal Growth

Copyright © 2014 by Jim R. Jacobs

Address all inquiries to:
Jim R. Jacobs, MSW, LCSW
10259 Ouray Street
Commerce City, CO 80022
Telephone (303) 288-2660
drivinglessonsforlife@gmail.com
www.drivinglessonsforlife.com

ISBN: 978-1-940984-40-7
Library of Congress Control Number: 2014941770

Editor: Tyler Tichelaar
Author Photo Credit: Rachel Eng
Cover and Interior Design: Angel Dog Productions

Published by Aviva Publishing
Lake Placid, NY
518-523-1320
www.avivapubs.com

Printed in the USA
First Edition

2 4 6 8 10 12

For additional copies visit:

www.drivinglessonsforlife.com

DEDICATION

For my beloved children. You are the driving force behind all I strive to do and to be. I love you.

ACKNOWLEDGMENTS

A special thank you to all the many who have believed in me, encouraged me, and helped me on the road of my life. I am grateful to all who have made this such a wonderful journey. I would especially like to thank:

Catherine Baird Pomeroy
Richard Southwick
G. Collin Smith
Andrea Krause
Margaret Lowe
Wendy Webster
Mark and Tresa Magnusson
Rex Johnson
Patrick Snow
Mark Glade
Rick Hill

CONTENTS

FOREWORD

Every now and then an author stumbles upon the book of a fellow writer and thinks, "Wow! I wish *I'd* thought of that!"

Driving Lessons for Life is such a book.

When Jim first introduced me to his manuscript, I knew he was on to something before I'd read a single paragraph. I was right.

In *Driving Lessons for Life*, Jim teaches valuable principles of happy and healthy living and becoming all you'd really like to be. Thankfully, Jim doesn't take the typical self-help or inspirational book approach. He crafts important life lessons into each chapter by relating a story or experience you've likely had behind the wheel of your car.

Each chapter offers a lesson, parable, or story, which connects you immediately to your own experiences. But it doesn't stop there. Jim takes the story and weaves an important principle of healthy and happy living. You'll gather insights and skills to help you achieve your goals, better live your life plan, and realize what you want most in life.

Sure, *Driving Lessons* may discuss what happens behind the wheel of a car, but you'll soon recognize that it's so much more. Every time you head down the road, you'll recall what you read and be reminded of an important principle. The way he carefully attaches these principles to your real-life experiences gives them more power to change you, to lift you, and to transform your goals to measurable success. Soon, constant reminders from your everyday drive will help you to apply what you've read and you'll be better equipped to navigate life and all the roads before you.

So hop in, buckle your seatbelt, and enjoy the ride. You've just enrolled in *Driving Lessons for Life*.

Jason
P.S. (I *still* wish I'd thought of that!)

Jason Wright is a *New York Times, Wall Street Journal* and *USA Today* best-selling author. He's a columnist for Fox News, *The Blaze, Deseret News*, and *Northern Virginia Daily*, and his articles have appeared in more than fifty other newspapers and magazines across the United States including *The Washington Times, The Chicago Tribune* and *Forbes*. He is the author of ten books that have been translated and sold around the world.

Jason is also a popular speaker on the topics of faith, the Christmas Jars movement, the Joy of Service, the lost art of letter writing, and many others. He has been seen on CNN, Fox News, C-SPAN, and on local television affiliates around the country.

For more information, visit: www.jasonfwright.com

NO LIMITS

Driving is a part of our everyday life. Today, the average person spends more time in the car than at any other time since the automobile's invention. We are driving all of the time. Yet, truth be told, most of us never think much about where we are going, how we got where we are, and the road we took on our journey. Today, most of us are rushing from one place to another, driving distracted, sometimes clueless, to all the happenings along the way. We blast our radios, talk on our Bluetooths, and do just about anything to check out. We are constantly moving but never sure we are really getting anywhere. Driving, and a lot of it, is what we do.

Think about it! Have you recently driven from one place to another, maybe from home to work, but you cannot remember anything happening along the way? Were you distracted, preoccupied, and stressed? Were you focused on something you wanted to do while driving, or were you being passively entertained by the radio or your iPod? In the last week, have you been so stressed with traffic, other drivers, or even inanimate traffic signs and signals that you yelled, cursed, or spoke out loud to them? Are you heading out on the roads of life without really knowing where you are going and what you are doing along the way? Are you *driving your life*, or is your life *really* driving you? If you are not sure, then this book is for you!

To be completely honest, I have been there! I have done my share of driving over the years, so I know it is too easy to check out, stress out, burn out, space out, or fly out of control when driving. I would believe you if you told me there are more drivers on the road now than at any other time in history because they are all on the road in front of me just when I need to get someplace in a hurry! I know what it is like to feel the frustration we now call "road rage." I know what it is like to be scared, stressed, overwhelmed, late, anxious, alone, and just wanting to get somewhere. Even more, I know what it feels like to have these challenges more than just on the highway. I have been like so many who are not sure where to go, what the best way to get there is, and how to make the most of the journey. I wrote this book because I wanted more. I know you want more too!

This book is all about driving lessons. Sure, you may learn something to help you improve your driving skills by reading it. However, this book is so much more. In this book, you will be reminded of common everyday experiences we all have when we get in a car. Then, a helpful life lesson will be presented to you. You will learn more about how to achieve your goals, become the kind of spouse, parent, or leader you would like to be, and how to handle your emotions better. You will read about ways to organize your life better, resolve challenges, and prioritize things that matter most. This will all happen as you read everyday examples of driving or traveling in a car. The stories will be even more powerful because you will remember them as you get behind the wheel of the car. Driving lessons will literally become life lessons every time you are in the car. You will reflect on them again and again, each time you encounter one of these events on your commute. Because the lessons will be connected to something you already do every day—driving somewhere—they will have more power to impact your life and produce changes for you. You will laugh and nod as you see yourself in some of these stories, and this will make them click even more for you. We all learn so well when we hear powerful stories we can immediately connect to our personal experience. That is exactly why this book will help you make powerful personal changes in your life. It is so connected to what you already do; it is so easily applicable to your life, and the lessons will help you make your life better. If you drive or ride in a car, you need this book.

I have written this book because I want to help you. I have spent over twenty years of my professional life helping individuals, couples, families, church leaders, and groups to make changes and improvements in their lives. For the past fifteen years, I have worked in close, personal contact with individuals who struggle to overcome huge personal challenges or obstacles, wrestle with abuse or addiction, and seek to be happy and fulfilled in life. Everywhere I go, I find people who are not sure where they are going, how to get away from the past, and how to make the most of the journey we call life. Challenges are real, and I have dedicated my career to helping alleviate those challenges. I have worked with thousands who want to make life better and realize their highest dreams. This book came about because I wanted to find a way to share some of those things with you. But I did not want it to be just another self-help or feel-good book. I wanted to find a way to weave it into your personal life so the lessons would be compelling, memorable, and impactful for you. With all of my experience guiding others on their personal roads, I knew I had more to share. I needed to reach you!

I know you probably have some reservations at this point. That is to be expected. Changing direction or even turning around in traffic can be really hard. It can be even more difficult in life. Yet I want to be your personal driving instructor. I want to help you get in the car, so to speak, and feel good about not only the direction you are going in your life, but all the stops along the way. I want you to get more out of your life's journey, and I want to take that road with you. As we take this journey together, you will clearly see I can help you with the challenges you face. Imagine yourself putting a "student driver" magnet or sign on your life. I will take the seat next to you and coach you along in these chapters. We will get to where you want to go and you will enjoy the journey getting there!

So let's get started. Unlike the signs you see on the street each day telling you how fast you can go, there are truly no limits here. You can go as fast or as slow as you want. You can read this book from front to back! You can just plop the book open and read where it lands. This book is designed to be read or listened to in the car, on the bus ride to work, on the toilet, or before you go to bed at night. You can read it how you want to read it. Even more, you won't find any exercises or places to fill in the blanks or write stuff down. You can, of course, choose to do that if you wish, but mostly, you will just want to read and reflect on these life lessons and make changes as they are right for you. Then, each and every time you drive somewhere, you will be reminded of what you learned. That way, you can come back to your old driving instructor to repeat the lesson again and again. The ideas and challenges will sink in and you will feel inspired to act. You can do this! No limits!

If I can be of any help to you along this journey, please do not hesitate to contact me for more driving lessons at www.DrivingLessonsForLife.com or DrivingLessonsForLife@gmail.com. I will offer you a complimentary, no cost, no obligation, free consultation.

No Limits!

"REAL LIVING
AND LIFE
COME FROM
THE PEOPLE,
THE
EXPERIENCES,
AND THE GOOD
WE SHARE
WITH OTHERS."

Chapter 1

A Car Is Just a Car

I started saving for a car when I was about twelve years old. I could not wait to drive. Three months before my sixteenth birthday, I paid $1,200 cash for my first car. I could not drive it legally for three more months. So it sat in front of the house until I turned sixteen and had my permit to drive. I was so excited to get on the road in my new car. When three months finally passed, I was in a large parking lot in my car with my stepfather. I was ready to go. That is when the lecture started *before* I was allowed to drive.

"A car is a car!" he told me.

Trying not to get frustrated, I plastered a fake smile on my face and acted interested. I had been going crazy for this moment for years. I would finally get to drive a car. The ride to this large parking lot had been torture, and now I had to listen to a lecture? He told me the seemingly obvious; a car is something to be used to get you from one place to another. That is all. Of course, my young, eager, testosterone-filled mind and body had other ideas. I was not really listening because I just wanted to drive. I had hoped he would stop talking and let me have the keys. He continued.

25

"A car is not a tow truck. It is not a race car. It is not a status symbol to impress people. It is not a place to live, to hide out, or even make out. It is a car."

I feigned more interest. He then spoke of my brother and some of his recent mishaps. Obviously, he was the reason I was getting this speech now. Thanks, Bro!

"People often forget the basic reason we have cars and what they are for," my stepfather droned on. "When we remember what a car is for, we drive more responsibly and are less likely to have problems. Many problems can be avoided by remembering just this one little thing—a car is just a car."

I was eventually given the keys to *my* car, and I began my first experiences driving. I was so excited and more nervous than I expected to be. I had to work very hard in those first lessons to drive as I was expected to drive. I probably did better than it felt, but it took a whole lot of concentration to learn all of the things required to be a good driver. It was some months before I drove comfortably, especially with an adult in the car watching my every move and commenting on it. Ultimately, I was driving alone and not really thinking about it much!

Interestingly, despite my apparent lack of interest in the "car is just a car" lecture when it was given, I have never forgotten that advice. In fact, just a few months ago, I repeated the same lecture to my daughter. A car really is just a car. Though I have not always followed that counsel, I have found it to be true, and I believe it was sound advice for driving and for life.

I learned after those early days of driving that it is quite easy to forget a car's true purpose. It was only a year later when I sold my first car and bought a classic Mustang. I probably spent thousands of dollars restoring my prized new car, adding new wheels, new paint, and more. I had to have the best stereo. I had to have the awesome speakers to go along with the best stereo. The car became my focus. I went to great lengths to buy the manuals from the manufacturer to know everything about the car. It became an object of focus for me. It also changed my car from a car to something else.

My car became all the things I was warned about in that first lesson. I began to look for status and prestige in my car. I was older than most kids in my grade, so I was cool because I was able to drive. When I became a Mustang owner, my status was elevated to king, or something like it. Heck, I even had a sunroof. I looked and felt like royalty when I turned that smooth crank and the roof dropped down and slid into its little compartment. I can still feel and hear the smooth purr as the crank turned and the cover slid open. Beautiful! I was really living high! People flocked to me to see my car, to listen to my stereo, and to watch me open the sunroof. They begged me to open it. My car was so cool! I was so cool!

I remember racing down the freeway at crazy speeds trying to catch the drag from the giant semi-truck in front of me. I could maneuver those turns and corners with precision. I was not being reckless. That would be irresponsible! I was just helping this car do what it was meant to do. A car like that, which looked like that, had to be driven like that—or so I believed. The attention and the turned heads was the prize. I had to have the prize. Fortunately for me, I was lucky and never turned the head of a police officer or, even worse, turned the car over! I had completely forgotten those first lessons.

When the adrenaline wears off, it becomes easy to see the risky behavior and danger that can come from forgetting what a car is. Much of life is like this. It is so easy to forget what certain things' real purposes are. We are seduced by commercials, Internet ads, and videos that lure us into a numb state of forgetting what really is true. You cannot turn on the television or see an advertisement without a promise that this or that product will give you something—satisfaction, peace, happiness, bliss, etc. It is easy to be deceived and believe that something is more than it really is. Could a car really be more than a car?

We are being deceived. Not only is a car just a car, but so many other things are just what they are. Shampoo is just shampoo. It just cleans your hair. Soda is just soda. It just quenches that thirst. Band-Aids are just Band-Aids, and so on! None of these things are friends, lovers, partners, associates, or coworkers. They are just things. None of the *things* of life bring us bliss, satisfaction, contentment, or any of the things we are told they will give us in subtle and not so subtle ways. They do what they are meant to do, and that is all. To be sure, these things are a nice part of life. However, and this is the point: They have no life. They are just the things that help get us along as part of real life. Real living and life come from the people, the experiences, and good we share with others. Real joy comes from family, good friends, and how we spend our time. This is where life comes from. A car is just a car. This advice is so good to remember.

"MOST LIFE DECISIONS ONLY NEED TO BE
MADE ONCE. WHEN WE HAVE, WITH
DETERMINED AND PRAYERFUL
RESOLVE, CHOSEN OUR
TRUE COURSE, WE ARE
BLESSED WITH PEACE
OF MIND AND
ASSURANCE WE
ARE GOING
TO ARRIVE
SAFELY."

Chapter 2

Getting in the Lane You Want to Be in and Staying in It

Driving is such a big part of my life. I drive my car pretty much every day of my life. It has become something essential. This is true for most people. We need our cars to get to work, to school, to soccer games, social events, church, and so much more. They take us to all the places we want and have to go to each day. What would we do without our cars?

In my almost daily experience of driving, I see something that reminds me of my first lessons behind the wheel. Every day, I see someone weaving in and out of traffic, cutting and darting in and out of as many lanes as are available. I see people change lanes at the last minute, swerve across multiple lanes, and repeat this process for miles. It is not likely that a day goes by without my seeing the lane swapping, which is such a part of our roadway life today. Everyone is moving from one lane to the other. We all do it at times.

I don't know all the reasons for the lane swapping we do when we drive. I imagine it is sometimes because we are late. Other times, we are impatient and frustrated. Maybe it is because we want to go faster so the dog can get a better tongue-wagging experience out the window! Occasionally, we have to change lanes because of debris in the road, potholes, or other hazards. Lane changing is part of the everyday drive of life. If you are on the road, expect to change lanes and see others changing lanes.

I don't change lanes very often when I drive and I do fine. I might just be boring like my kids tell me. I might just be old fashioned or just old, but I don't move around too much when I drive from one place to the other. To get where I am going, I find myself following the sage advice of my stepfather:

"Get in the lane you want to be in and stay in it!"

What great advice for life! In driving, I have learned to plan and think ahead about where I am going. Then, I get in the lane I want to be in or need to be in to get to that place, and I drive. It does not matter much what obstacles or vehicles I encounter; I choose my lane and stick to it. I know which lane takes me where I want to go and I stay in it. Even if I am not completely sure of where I am going, I apply this strategy. If I have to turn left ahead some distance, I quickly get to the left lane and stay in it until I get to my turn. I repeat this process until I arrive—get in the lane I need to be in and stay there.

Many (if not most) life decisions only need to be made once. For instance, you can decide today to go to college, be honest in all you do, never do drugs, and more. You only have to decide these things one time. That's right! One time is all it takes. It is wise and helpful to consider carefully what you want and make the choice now. Then, you will not have to make the decision in the moment—in crisis—when it is so much harder to make. When you firmly choose your direction and the steps it takes to get there (or stay away from there), life is so much easier to navigate. When we have, with determined and prayerful resolve, chosen our true course, we are blessed with peace of mind and assurance we are going to arrive safely and without as much trouble. Decide early and carefully which lane you want to be in, and stay in it. That will get you there!

"MANY OF LIFE'S CHALLENGES CAN BE MET MORE READILY IF WE ARE FOCUSED ON WHAT IS AHEAD OF US."

Chapter 3

Driving Down the Road

It has become commonplace for people to run red lights, stop or swerve quickly, and otherwise drive erratically. When we are in a hurry to get places, we often become careless and even reckless in our driving. I hate pulling up to the scene of an accident and wondering whether the whole thing could have been prevented by a different practice. Also, it seems normal for people to have to make quick changes because they missed the merge or yield sign, did not see the construction zone, or some other indication of a need to alter their course. Again, I wonder whether these last-minute changes could have been avoided. Is there some practice we could implement to prevent this or minimize it? It is called driving down the road.

When I was learning to drive, I was told to "drive down the road." I had no idea what this meant. I thought I *was* driving down the road. Then, my stepfather pointed off in the distance. He told me I should always be thinking about and noticing what is ahead of me. He told me if I would just try to notice the conditions ahead, it would give me time to plan, to prepare, and even avoid much of what is out there that could harm me or my car. So he pointed out to me the traffic lights in the distance, the large hole in the road, construction signs, and more. They were all still quite a way away. Yet I noticed something as I attended to what was down the road; it became easier to maneuver through what was coming. I noticed over time I did not have to make quick adjustments, sudden lane changes, or erratic moves. As I watched ahead of me—well ahead of me—I was calmer and felt more assurance and confidence in where I was going. Driving became easier, less scary, and more relaxed.

As on the road, so in life. We need to take the long view. We need to look well ahead of our current place on the path and see what is in store for us. Many of life's challenges can be met more readily if we are focused on what is ahead of us. There are many missteps we would not make, many pitfalls we would avoid, if we tried to maintain a view of what lies farther ahead of us.

On many occasions, I find myself asking, "Where will this choice lead me?" Every so often, I can recognize a choice that may be good to make in the present, but that would not turn out well for my or others' benefit in the long run—down the road. Even more, when contemplating my life's direction, I have found great benefit in asking, "What things am I doing right now, which, if continued, might cause me to be off course in ten years?" It is powerful to look ahead, farther down the road, and really examine what is there.

Often, I have been able to see the unwise course current decisions or actions (and even inactions) have placed me on. This quick realization has allowed me more easily to change my trajectory and improve my path. I believe many hard experiences and challenges can be avoided by driving down the road. So take the long view and see what is down there. It may help more than you know.

"DETERMINE EARLY ON TO HEED THE SIGNS OF CONSCIENCE THAT TELL US WE ARE ABOUT TO VEER OFF. MAKE THE DECISION TO KEEP RIGHT."

Chapter 4

Keeping Right

It just happened a few weeks ago. My daughter and I were off on a "Daddy Date" and we had to pass through a construction zone. To help us navigate through the cones and constructions signs was the all-too-familiar sign: an arrow veering to the right around an odd-shaped cone thing and the words: "Keep right." So we followed the cones and sign to the right. We made it safely through the work zone.

I wonder whether we really need those signs. I mean it seems pretty obvious to me to follow the cones and signs. Fluorescent orange obstacles surround the path I am supposed to follow. It kind of seems like it would be difficult (and maybe even take some extra work) to get around to the left where I am not supposed to be. Yet the other part of me knows the reason we have these kinds of signs. Sometime in the past, someone was not looking ahead and found himself on the left side of the road. In a construction zone, the mistake of going to the left could be harmful or fatal to many people. It could thrust them directly into fast-moving traffic heading the other way. Keeping to the right is an obvious wise choice. I am guessing that more than once, cars have been driven to the left into potential disaster. Keeping right is a good move. I love the sign.

We live in a world where every day the news media is trumpeting the story of another person who told a lie, cheated on a test, or stole something from another. We read of people cheating on exams. We hear of others who cheated in sporting events, athletic competitions, or other special events. Even more harmful, we come face-to-face with people cheating other people. People in trusted positions, be they spouses, leaders, or role models, are often found to be guilty of cheating or lying. It is sad to hear so many daily accounts of such conduct. It is sad we are so intrigued by it. I think it is because, inside, we all can see a small sign from our conscience that says we should "Keep right."

Did you ever stop to think about these people who cheat? I am willing to bet that not one of them started out in his or her career, competition, or marriage with the intent to lie, cheat, or steal. No one does this! Each athlete was at one point working hard to build muscle, speed, or endurance. Another person studied for hours, joined a study group, or hired a tutor. Still, someone else pledged love and loyalty forever. So how then did they move from a place of effort and integrity to a place of dishonor and humiliation? Most likely, the cause is related to a series of decisions not to keep right. One small decision. "No one will know" and "Just once" come to mind and mouth. Suddenly, one small decision leads to another. A path begins to form and we are on a path and road to disaster we never intended.

The way to prevent this is clear. We make the decision to keep right. We determine early on to heed the signs of conscience that tell us we are about to veer off. We might even imagine a sign in our mind in those moments that reads "Keep right" and decide to do exactly that. If, by chance, we find we are already off course, we can quickly get right and stay there. The best course is always to keep right.

"THINGS
THAT GROW
AND MOVE SLOWLY
TEND TO LIVE LONGER.
THIS IS TRUE FOR TREES,
AND IT IS TRUE FOR PEOPLE.
THERE IS SO MUCH LIFE TO
BE LIVED AND ENJOYED.
IF WE ARE GOING
TOO FAST,
WE WILL
MISS
IT."

Chapter 5

If You Want to Live to See 100, Don't Look for It on Your Speedometer

When I was about ten years old, I was the typically awkward boy who liked to tell bad jokes, and I laughed at the silliest and grossest of things. For my birthday that year, my stepsisters gave me *The World's Largest Joke Book*. It was about sixteen inches long and at least three inches thick with vivid colored pages. Immediately, they wished they had not purchased this gift for me. I was already dangerous on my own with jokes. Now I had hundreds of pages of jokes and one-liners to fire at everyone I saw. They regretted giving me this book for many years. The title of this chapter was one of the many things I found in the book. I did not get its meaning at the time, or even why it was in a joke book, but I have thought of it often since then.

Believe it or not, I don't go to many movies. I do notice the trailers, however. It is interesting to me how many movies involve speeding cars and fast drivers. I remember from my youth the Cannonball Run series. There also was *Smokey and the Bandit*. Since then, we have had *Days of Thunder*, *Speed*, *Drive*, and *Gone in Sixty Seconds*. The Fast and Furious series has been a huge moneymaker. More recently, we have had

The Need for Speed and *Rush*. Pixar even got into the mix of portraying fast cars in its animated-feature movie, *Cars*. We are infatuated with driving fast. We want to watch cars go fast. Then, we want to drive our own cars fast. What is it about speed that we need?

It may be just me, but all of these fast-driving, speed, and thrill-seeking movies involve young and good-looking people. I get it! A movie about grandpa speeding around the corner at thirty-five miles an hour in his dirty, orange Plymouth Duster is probably not going to do much for anyone. Bright and fast cars are supposed to be driven by young and beautiful people. Speed is younger people stuff! However, I know many of these movies are being watched by older men like me who long ago traded the souped-up Mustangs of their youth for a beat-up Saturn sedan or a mini-van. I cannot go too fast in my current car. It starts to shake at about 55 miles per hour. Anything much faster and I will get a teeth-rattling ride where I will either have to stop and go to the bathroom or risk that something will fall off the car. Older people, like me in our older and slower cars, just cannot handle fast. The older I get, the more I want to slow down. I am starting to realize how much I may have missed in my youthful speeding through life. Things that grow and move slowly tend to live longer. This is true for trees, and it is true for people. There is so much life to be lived and enjoyed. If we are going too fast, we will miss it. Slowing down makes it more enjoyable, and no doubt safer, to drive the roads of life. I want to slow down and soak up all there is to see. I want to enjoy scenery, meet people I have always wanted to meet, and take in history and beauty everywhere. I don't want to miss anything or anyone beautiful, interesting, or original. I can find all of this and more everywhere I go, if I am going slow enough to see it. I don't know whether I want to live to see 100, but I do want to move safely and securely through whatever years of life I have left. I don't feel the need for speed. I have had enough of that stuff. I want to see all I can see and make sure I am around to enjoy it all.

"IT
HAS BEEN SAID
YOU CAN TELL A LOT
ABOUT SOMEONE BY
HOW HE HANDLES
THE LITTLE THINGS
THAT CAN
FRUSTRATE US."

Chapter 6

Drive Like Hell and You'll Get There

Not too long ago, I attended a presentation from an expert on psychopathology who was teaching us about why people do really scary and horrific things. At one point in the presentation, he said something like: "In the United States, you are going to see so many interesting things on the road because we have a random sample of the population. So there are going to be some real nuts out there." He then explained more about the phenomenon of road rage and other seemingly "psycho" behaviors we may encounter on the road. Just our luck, because most people in the U.S. can and will drive a car at some time, we will always be "blessed" with interesting experiences! Some of those experiences will be downright disturbing. My youngest daughter and I experienced one such incident on a Saturday afternoon lunch date.

We were headed to a favorite restaurant together. We had to turn left onto the highway. We pulled into the left-hand turn lane behind a very large box truck. Since we were in my small sedan, we could not see around the truck. Apparently, the light changed as the truck started to move forward. As we approached the intersection, I was unable to determine whether the arrow to turn was still green, so I slowed down to be safe. I allowed enough distance to wait and see whether it was safe to make the left turn. Waiting, I saw the arrow turn yellow and red, so I gently stopped at the light to wait for the next cycle. Then I looked behind me.

In my mirror, I could clearly see the man behind me. He was yelling and pounding on the dashboard. I could not tell for sure since I was viewing through the mirror, but there appeared to be a stream of expletives coming out of his mouth. He then took off his hat and pounded it on the dashboard of his car. He was obviously very angry at me for not making the turn. He pulled his hair, thrashed his body wildly about, and continued to slam his hat against the dash with his other hand. I became frightened a moment later when he opened his door as if to get out and come up to me. I quickly reached to lock the door and saw him get back in his car with a slamming sound. He continued to rant and rave, alternating between pulling on his hair and smacking the dashboard repeatedly. Then, when the light changed again, he squealed around me and waved at me with one finger. He then raced erratically on to the highway. My heart was racing with a little anxiety about the circumstance, but I sighed in relief that he was now on his way. Imagine my surprise when just a few moments down the road, we saw him sitting at a red light waiting for it to change. You guessed it! He was still throwing his tantrum. It was just not his day!

I don't really know for sure, but I think I had just witnessed what some scriptural accounts, describing hell and those sent there, call "weeping and wailing and gnashing of teeth." I was just driving safely on the road to lunch with my daughter. I like to think I was in control of myself behind the wheel of my car. For this man, it was a completely different experience. He was out of control and it showed. He was hijacked by a rage I believe most would consider irrational and unreasonable. He lost it! He could not control his outward circumstances, including the driver and lights in his path on his way. Therefore, his life became a kind of hell-in-the-moment because he obviously could not control himself.

So much about life is beyond our control. Each day, we are all faced with obstacles and events that, if we let them, will cause us stress and frustration. Many of these are really of small consequence (like missing the green turn arrow). Others may be larger and carry the potential of greater impact. Yet we always retain the ability to control and compose ourselves. We are given the capacity to choose our thoughts and actions. No other creatures under the heavens have such capacity given to them. It is telling how we respond to these little frustrations and unfortunate delays in getting what we want or where we want to go. It has been said you can tell a lot about someone by how he handles the little things that can frustrate us. Do we respond as the man behind my daughter and I? What little things upset us and get us to act in hellish ways? If we let it, there is much about life to take us down a dark and scary road, feeling miserable. We also can choose to relax, remind ourselves things will be okay, and go forward with some composure. Surely, the loss of self-control, especially in the most insignificant of circumstances, reflects a lot about who we are and what we value. Truly, the greatest control is self-control. To lose that really seems to produce a kind of hell—a place I want to avoid.

Chapter 7

Going Nowhere Fast

I am pretty sure I am not alone in this feeling, but I hate driving in congested traffic. I dislike this experience so much that I have even moved to another neighborhood to avoid it. I cannot think of anyone I know who enjoys being stuck in traffic. I am pretty positive if I did find someone who enjoyed it, I would have him committed. So if you enjoy being stuck in traffic jams, better not tell me because as a clinical social worker, I actually have the professional license and ability to have you locked up! Straitjackets anyone? "I love traffic jams and rush hour," said no one ever!

The only perk of being stuck in traffic, for me, has been to observe other people. Many years ago, I had an opportunity to see something unique. I was on a three-lane highway headed home in the evening rush hour. Traffic was crawling along, but we were moving. Ahead of me was a sharp-looking convertible with a driver who was obviously in a hurry. He was jerking in and out of lanes, switching every few minutes. I had chosen to be in the left-hand lane and was slowly crawling forward. He kept switching. The traffic was going so slowly that I could not help but watch him and his reactions. What happened over time on this long commute home surprised me and angered him. The more he switched lanes, the farther back he got. So I literally caught up and was even with him. Then, as he continued to swerve in and out of lanes, he moved farther back. Soon, he was no longer beside me, but farther behind me. Now I was spying on his antics in my rear-view mirror. He continued to move back and forth, in and out, slowly getting so far behind me that I could no longer watch him. Eventually, I moved forward and never saw him again. The experience, however, left a mark on me and helped me to learn an important lesson about life.

Often in life, we confuse movement with progress. Like this anxious driver, we are moving, but we are really going nowhere fast. We don't always recognize this phenomenon when it is happening because we are stuck on the fact that we are moving. I don't know, but it seemed this man was completely unaware of his lack of progress. It was obvious to me. Yet perhaps he noticed and thought if he continued his effort, it would eventually help him. Maybe he was chasing his losses and thinking, "*This time* I will break free and really move forward." I can only imagine his thinking and feeling. Nevertheless, he was not moving forward in spite of his frantic efforts to do so.

How often do we find ourselves approaching life in the same way this driver approached the evening rush hour? We get to moving in a certain direction. Yet, we are not realizing the objectives we had intended with that movement. I have seen many people desperately trying to change their own behaviors or the behavior of a family member, and the actions they are taking are not moving them forward. The best example I can think of was one time when I was talking to a mother frustrated with her daughter. She lamented having her daughter not respond to her efforts to correct her behavior. She described all kinds of movement. She said she had tried rewards, incentives, bribes, taking away privileges, lectures, and more recently, she had resorted to yelling and threats. She agonized over the lack of progress and noted feelings of being completely out of control as a result of her frustration. She disclosed being afraid she might even do something she would regret. She told me it had not always been this way, and she was frantic to discover how to get things back on track. This fear is what prompted her to seek assistance from me. She was at her wit's end.

After spending enough time with her to assess what was going on and validate her emotions and level of distress, I began to inquire more about what was happening. I was looking for some examples of the supposedly intractable problem. The central issue she wanted to discuss was getting her daughter to clean her room. She told me she used to be able just to ask and her daughter would respond. She was even cheerful. Then, as the daughter got older, asking did not seem to work anymore. So Mom "turned up the volume." When her daughter did not respond right away, Mom said she started getting busy with all these approaches to help her daughter get her room clean. Now she felt she had exhausted all of her options. No amount of effort could produce the desired result. All this movement was not moving her and her daughter's relationship forward. Or so she thought.

I then asked her the key question, "When *does* your daughter clean her room?" She surprised me with her reply, "Oh, she always cleans her room for me." I queried "I don't understand." She said, "She will clean it for me if I ask her, but I don't want to have to ask her!" Then she added that she wanted her daughter not only to clean her room without being asked, but "to be happy about it." Again in frustration, she whined, "I just don't know what to do!"

"So are you telling me your daughter will clean her room 100 percent of the time if you just ask her?"

"Yes! Every time! It is terrible! I want her to do it on her own and not complain about it!"

I prodded a little now. I asked her whether she would be willing to look at this a little bit differently and consider changing her present course of action. I told her I believed her actions were getting her nowhere fast. She was upset and her daughter was upset. Neither liked the result. We agreed one of the primary objectives was to get the room clean and have her daughter be responsible. She also admitted that her daughter might never become cheerful about this chore. The next thing I said to her surprised her so much that I almost chuckled at her reaction.

"So if your daughter will clean her room every time you ask her, would you be willing to consider this a great success and just learn to be okay with asking?" I reminded her of how high a success rate every time would be and praised her obvious good parenting. I talked to her about how nice it would be if children did things because they liked to and wanted to do them, but perhaps that goal was not realistic for a teenager. She was astounded.

"I never thought of it that way! I guess I have not really been getting anywhere with the other approach." She left the appointment boosted in mood and did not come back. This session was one of the few times when I have only had to meet with someone one time. Once she realized her approach was getting her nowhere fast, she quickly changed and moved forward.

So if you find yourself not making progress, the answer may not be just to add more movement. Slow down or even stop. Look around and determine where you really want to go and how you are going about getting there. Evaluate your movements, and if they are not producing positive change or growth, try something else. If you are seemingly going nowhere fast, stop moving until you are sure the movement is causing you to go forward.

Chapter 8

Following the Lines

For many years of my career, I have had the privilege of traveling by car to many different locations. Often on these work trips, I would travel in the early morning hours. I will never forget the sunrise over Jacksonville that I observed one morning. I will also never forget the frozen road and "new" animals I saw on my long-stretch drive between Casper and Riverton, Wyoming. There have been so many sights to see when I drive. I sometimes miss the scenery of this great country. Still, this responsibility to be on the road has also meant that I have had to drive in all kinds of weather. I have pushed on through the fog in Gainesville, Florida; persevered through crazy rain in Dayton, Florida; braved snowstorms over the pass in Monument, Colorado; and had many more weather experiences on the road. Most of the time, I have felt very safe since I am a careful and conservative driver. A few times, I have been terrified and wondered whether I would make it safely to my destination. The two most frightening experiences have been during downpours in Florida and during white-out snowstorms in central Wyoming. I feel blessed that I have been protected on the road and have made it safely wherever I have gone.

I have noticed a couple of decisions I have made when facing various road and weather conditions. The first decision has been to press forward and keep going. I have yet to stop and "wait out" a storm. I don't know all of my motivations in these cases. The one seemingly most pressing is a desire to get home. In each case where I was facing terrible weather, I was at the end of a long trip and very eager to get home. I am not really advocating this approach. However, I have been careful in these situations and probably lucky that the decision to press on did not cause me harm. I hope I would be wise enough to stop and wait if it were really necessary. I guess I have justified those past decisions because I made it home.

The second decision relates to the first. I decided to focus on the lines on the road. I believe if I ever found myself driving and I could no longer see any lines, I would be more likely to stop. In each of the cases (even the most terrifying ones), I could still see lines on the road. As long as I could see the lines, I would slowly push forward toward home. I had something clear to guide me and help me on my way. If I just followed the lines, I knew I would make it safely through the storm.

What are the lines we should follow in life to navigate safely through the storms that most certainly will come? How should we determine which way to go when hard times come? I find a focus on some fixed principles has really helped me. These fixed "lines" have helped me to make it down the roads of life. Maybe one example will show how this works.

My mother wanted her kids to be honest. We were punished for a lot of wrong things kids do, but the severest punishment was for not being honest. I realized quickly that being honest was a rule worth following (to avoid the punishment and because it was a good thing), and I determined I would strive to be honest in all I chose to do. It has been a challenge, but I truly believe in being honest. I determined it was the right course of life for me. Thus, it was not too long before my mom may have regretted pushing honesty so much. We were checking out at the store. My mom had chosen (for many reasons) not to have our phone number printed on her checks. So as we checked out, the pimple-faced cashier asked her for the number. My mom gave her a fake number. I was quick to speak up and most insistent when my mother shushed me about "the mistake." We quickly departed. Just as we were pulling out of the parking lot, the adolescent clerk stopped us and asked for the correct number. My mom flushed. I thought it better not to say anything about honesty at this point (although I wanted to).

I began to get a reputation for honesty. We still have a classic family photograph where you can tell I am trying to tell my mother a lie. I just cannot do it. Family members will resist telling me about surprise parties and other situations that require "white lies" because I will probably not be able to make it through any questioning. My siblings hated it if we were engaged (and caught) in any kind of sibling-group misbehavior. Mom knew whom to ask first. She knew I would crack. I never understood why either of my siblings would still lie when I had already been forced to spill the beans. I was not good at dishonesty. I have found this to be an incredibly good thing, and one of those lines I can follow throughout my life. I have not been perfect, but I strive to stay in and follow that line.

What lines might you want to put in place and strive to follow in your life? What is really important to you? What topics do you really have a passion for? Are you really big into personal responsibility? Integrity? A full-day's work for a full-day's pay? Doing random acts of kindness? You could make these the guiding lines by which you navigate your life. Some years ago, I wrote a series of belief statements to guide me. Each statement started with "I believe in..." and then ended with something I strongly believed. These "I believe" statements end with my convictions about what kind of father I want to be, my physical health, my spiritual health, my personal conduct, and more. This has been a charter document for me, helping me to stay centered on what matters most to me in my life. In a very real way, these are the lines to guide me on my personal journey.

You could do something similar. Sit down and reflect on what really matters to you and what you really believe in. Pull out a piece of paper or your tablet and record some of these thoughts. Work with and edit them until you get to the key items for you. Then make these your guidelines for how you move forward each day. You might be surprised by what happens in your life and what challenges and obstacles you can get through as you follow these lines.

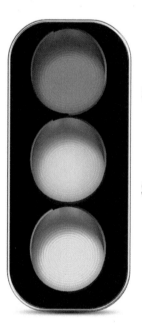

"WHAT SEEMED SO SIMPLE AND INSIGNIFICANT AT ONE POINT LITERALLY SAVED ME, NOT ONCE, BUT THREE TIMES IN A ROW."

Chapter 9

10 and 2

Driver's Education instructors tell us to imagine our car's steering wheel is a clock and our hands are to be placed at 10 and 2 for the best and safest driving. They assure us we will be more in control of our vehicle if we have both hands placed firmly in these key spots. They will warn eager students about other favored positions. They may even name them. We have the "relaxed-9-only" where your left arm is hanging out the window and you lightly hold the wheel with your left hand. You may have the "all-too-casual-6" where you are barely touching the steering wheel with a couple of fingers while your arms rest in your lap. They will sternly warn against "the knee-press" where you have no hands on the wheel so you can do some unsafe thing while your knee or leg handles the maneuvering. The safest way to drive is 10 and 2.

I must confess I have wondered about this direction. I have even thought to myself, "Hey! I could get there thirty minutes faster if I placed my hands at 9:45 and 2:15!" Other times, I have surely been casual about where my hands are placed when I drive. I am proud to say, however, that most of the time, my hands are where they are supposed to be—

10 and 2! I once had an experience that illustrated for me the importance of this instruction.

I was the keynote speaker at a meeting in St. Petersburg, Florida. At the time, I lived in Orlando, Florida, and I had to make the two to three hour drive to the meeting. I was a bit late in leaving for the meeting (but I did not switch my hands to 9:45 and 2:15 to make up the time!), so I was a little stressed. I hopped on the freeway, quickly moved to the left lane for speed, and started on my way. My hands were securely placed at 10 and 2, and I was making good time. Fortunately for me, my hands were in the best and safest place because I was soon to have, not one, but three experiences to show me the wisdom of this direction.

As I sped quickly along at about seventy-five miles an hour, I witnessed the car in front of me quickly swerve to the right. Then, it was my turn. There was a large, coiled rope or chain of some kind in the road that would have surely caused an accident if hit. I made it around the object. My heart started that frantic racing thing it does in moments like this. It takes great effort to calm down as my mind reflects, "That was a close one." A quick prayer of thanks and I pressed on. Hands still at 10 and 2.

Then, to my surprise (true story!), there was a mattress in the middle of the road, approaching me at a very fast speed! Eek! I had just moments to plan to get around this new obstacle, quickly make the adjustment, and hope it worked out. This was one of those times when you just want to close your eyes and hope it works like it always does for the cartoon characters. Well, I did not close my eyes, but fortunately, I was able

to swerve around the mattress and get back in the lane I needed to be in. My heart was pounding so loudly in my chest
that it sounded like the nice woofers in the back window of
the car. I could have done a good rap to this beat. I didn't, but
I could have. I continued on, amazed at these two experiences
and grateful for my fortune in avoiding the worst.

I pressed on and found myself coming around the bend, able
to see St. Petersburg on the horizon. I was still making good
time when I came upon a work truck filled with tools and
accessories. To my horror, the ladder on the back of this truck
broke free from its restraints and flew off the back of the truck,
careening toward my car. Pure reaction at this point—I jerked the wheel to the right and around the deadly projectile. It
was just like one of those scenes in an action movie. Seriously.
It was as if I watched the ladder go by in slow motion, missing my car and my windshield by inches. At this point, I was
completely shaken up inside. My hands were trembling and
I was thinking either someone did not want me to go to this
meeting or this was the deadliest stretch of highway around.
I was also thinking I was so very fortunate not to have had
an accident (of either kind at this point, if you know what I
mean!). This drive was unbelievable. Luckily, I had no other
incidents for the remainder of my trip.

What made the difference? There is no doubt in my mind
about what happened. My choice to follow the safety advice
protected me from certain harm and accident. What seemed
so simple and insignificant at one point literally saved me,
not once, but three times in a row. I got the heavenly message
being sent to me: Follow safe practices. This advice has been
something I sincerely strive to do. We live in a world with

many dangers where mishaps, accidents, and harm can come to us. It would be well for us to do all we can to follow known safety guidelines. Many an injury and accident could be prevented if we just followed the best and safest practices known to us. I laugh like everyone else at some of the warnings. I love, just like everyone else, comedy routines that poke fun at various safety reviews. Yet I strive to do my best to prevent any mishap or accident I am able to prevent. It is true that most accidents are preventable if we would just be careful. It is tempting to cut corners, tell ourselves, "Nothing bad will happen to me," and lull ourselves into a false sense of security. We may even say, "I have done this 100 times and I don't need to worry." Before we know it, our hands have slipped to 9:45 and 2:15 and we are not as prepared. A little more time passes, with us becoming more casual and complacent, and soon our hands are at relaxed 9, 6, or not even on the wheel at all. We may even seem to be safe and okay in these moments, but why take the chance? It is better to arrive alive and safe than face the terrible tragedy of an accident. When we can, we should do all we can to practice all of the safety advice we have at our disposal. When we do, we cannot be assured we will be safe from all harm, but we can claim peace in knowing we did the best we could. Most accidents will be prevented by this choice. I believe it is a wise one.

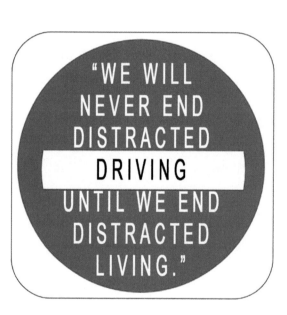

Chapter 10

Taking Those Safe Driving Pledges

As a father, I feel it is my duty to do all I can to annoy my children. I consider it one of my most important responsibilities. So I seek to do anything I can to embarrass them, make them blush, or feel annoyed with expressions of love from me. One thing that really seems to annoy them is when I do not jump up to answer my phone or text messages right when my phone beeps or rings. They go to great lengths to tell me my phone is ringing. They will carry it across the house to me. When I act uninterested, it frustrates them.

"Aren't you going to answer it?" they will ask me. Then they look horrified when I tell them I am not going to answer it and I point out whatever it is I am doing at the moment. Even if I am not doing anything at all, I will often not take the phone call or respond to the text message. For me, it is about learning to be the master over my decisions and actions—not letting the phone decide for me is part of that mastery. I have made the decision not to let momentary things distract me from the things that matter most to me at the time.

I have done my share of driving over the years. I have witnessed so many ways drivers are distracted on the road. Once on the freeway, I observed a man reading the newspaper. He had the paper fully unfolded and opened—completely covering the steering wheel. His hands were at 9 and 3 and he was getting his daily news. From my vantage point, it seemed he could barely see over the top of the paper. I have seen tons of women putting on make-up. Just yesterday, I saw a woman curling her eyelashes. I have seen women painting their nails with the bottle of polish precariously placed on the dashboard, one hand spread wide open, and the other holding the brush. I have seen people changing clothes, reading books, kissing their companions, and more. Of course, I regularly see people on their phones, talking and texting. We all have seen people weaving or wandering from their lanes. Distracted driving is something so very common.

I have been encouraged by many of the efforts to get people to commit to safe driving. These "safe driving pledges" are an important thing. They are all basically the same in their message. They encourage the driver to make a commitment not to use a cell phone to talk or text while driving. Some of these messages correctly indicate that whatever is on the other end of the call can wait. Others commit the driver to being completely safe. Others tout the growing body of research on distracted driving and promote arriving alive to your destination. All of these messages are good, and I myself, have taken a safe driving pledge. I do not use my phone for any reason when driving. Usually, it is in my briefcase or my back pocket. The pledge not to drive while distracted is an important one. However, I believe a pledge is missing the real problem. It is treating the symptoms and not the cause.

I believe we will continue to be distracted in our driving as long as we are distracted so much in our lives. In short, the problem is not distracted driving—it is distracted living. We spend so much of our lives in distraction. We cannot go anywhere without hearing phones chirping or beeping. We get on the Internet and have pop-ups, reminders, task lists, and more. Much of today's living reminds me of my brief time working for a fast-food restaurant as a teen—something was always beeping somewhere. We have all seen it. Go to your favorite sit-down restaurant and watch the people. I promise you will see people who likely went to this restaurant to spend some quality time together, yet they are talking or texting, scrolling or social networking. They are physically present, but too distracted truly to interact with the people in front of them. Some have joked that we don't need movies or shows about the walking dead or zombies because they are already here—numbed behind our cell phones.

Many of life's greatest joys come from being fully engaged in our purposes. We hear psychologists and religious leaders talking about being present. It has become popular to talk about mindfulness and learning to engage fully in the task at hand. More and more research is being conducted on the human proclivity to distraction and how it affects us in so many negative ways. An old proverb states, "If you chase two rabbits, you will catch neither one." More and more, we are hearing of the need to simplify, eliminate distractions, slow down, and do one thing at a time. This is wise advice. When I reflect on my greatest and happiest moments, I realize they all involved being fully present and engaged in some activity, whether it was performing in or attending a concert, playing with my kids, or worshipping together with friends and family. When I am fully connected, I am more fulfilled. My level of engagement is often connected to my level of satisfaction and enjoyment in the activity. It is not always easy to stay focused, but the greatest moments come not from being pulled in every direction all at once, but from fully engaging in one meaningful activity at a time.

So I advocate for safe driving pledges where we promise not to be distracted. I would also encourage us to take a real, living pledge. Let's make a commitment to live without distraction. Let's make a pledge to spend real time with someone. You could start by creating some technology free zones in your home and life. You could leave your phone in the car when you go out to eat with your family. You could wait to answer an email or text message when you are with others. Distraction is a powerful thing. It can make us place relatively meaningless things over the things that matter most. It is really easy to get distracted by something chirping, ringing, or beeping right now. So take the pledge today, and don't respond. It will bring joyful fruits.

"WE MAY MISS SOMETHING GRAND IF WE TOO QUICKLY REJECT OTHERS' COUNSEL AND CORRECTION. EVEN MORE, WE MAY FIND OURSELVES LOST AND ALONE IF WE ARE NOT WILLING TO SEEK HELP AND ACCEPT IT WHEN IT COMES."

Chapter 11

Back-Seat Drivers

Most drivers seem to hate back-seat drivers. This situation happens when the person in the back seat starts to give instructions and directions to the person driving the car. Most commonly, the driver is annoyed by this intrusion into his or her freedom. Most drivers seem to react defensively to any commentary or help from behind. I remember arguments in my family because someone in the back seat tried to offer some helpful advice to the driver. I have seen major contention erupt over a helpful suggestion from the back. Feeling like someone is trying to control them, drivers resist and refuse to hear helpful words. Why do we hate back-seat drivers so much? I believe it is because we have not learned to love correction and direction from others.

We all seem to have a need to believe we are doing things right. We want to be in control, and we seem to resent anyone who hints that we may not have all the answers or be doing everything correctly. We seem to kick against anything that does not appear to be our own thoughts or our own ideas. We want to decide where we are going, we want to drive the way we want to drive, and we want to do it in our very own way. We don't want any comments or help from the "cheap seats" or "the peanut gallery." We want to be left alone to do our own thing. I am not sure this desire is always such a wise one.

I believe we all should seek help from the back seat more often. We could actually ask for help from those behind us. Then we could accept their help with a gracious and simple "Thank you." The truth is many wise and wonderful people are all around us, wherever we go. Metaphorically speaking, important people are sitting in the back seat on any journey we take. Even more, we miss the blessings of different perspectives if we don't open ourselves to them. Often, those sitting in different seats, viewing things from different angles, have something profound to offer. We may miss something grand if we too quickly reject others' counsel and correction. Even more, we may find ourselves lost and alone if we are not willing to seek help and accept it when it comes.

Several years ago, my family was traveling home from a wedding. It was a joy to be together with all of our family, celebrating such an occasion. On the drive home, we encountered a severe thunderstorm that almost blinded me as the driver. We crawled slowly along, and tensions were high in the car and seemingly all around us because of the weather and traffic. My wife, seated next to me, was trying to offer help. I was trying to focus on the road. I was irritated by her interruptions, and she was expectedly frustrated with my lack of response. Then, from the back seat, our young daughter said, "Why don't we say a prayer?" My wife thanked her for her faithful comment and commended her wise choice. My wife asked her to say a prayer. All my family members (except for me—I was driving!) bowed their heads, folded arms and hands, and closed their eyes while my daughter said a sweet prayer asking for safety and peace in our drive home. What came next was sweet peace, and we thanked her and moved forward.

When we look for it, there is much we can gain from those all around us—even those in the back seat. We need each other. We need to open up to accept and support each other. We need to invite those around us to offer help, feedback, and even correction. When we respond with gratitude, we can be assured of kinder help and support. We don't always have to go the way others tell us to go, but there is power in being open, listening, and accepting direction from the back seat. Like a child's suggestion of prayer in a scary time on the road, there is much wisdom and help available—even in the back seat.

Chapter 12

Front-Seat Drivers

So we know about back-seat drivers, but it is not uncommon to have a front-seat driver as well. This is when the person in "shotgun" (the passenger seat) assists with the driving. Like the back-seat driver, this person may give out helpful comments and advice. However, the front-seat driver often resorts to other methods to assist the driver of the vehicle. These methods can include stomping on the imaginary brake on his or her side, bracing against the dashboard, and clinging to "the chicken handle" on the ceiling. This person is often known for white-knuckling it and all kinds of verbal gestures indicating a variety of emotions. While not limited to women, most commonly this kind of driver is of the female-type and is known by the title of wife or mother. The degree to which she engages in front-seat driving is often determined by the gender and teenage-ness of the driver. The front-seat driver typically cannot resist being of "help" in all the above ways.

Over the years, the female, front-seat driver has taken quite a lot of abuse. She is fun to make fun of, and men, in general, are insensitive to her plight. Often, when the well-meaning, front-seat, imaginary-brake-pounding wife resorts to these methods, she is met by a defensive and irritated husband.

Many a fight in the car has erupted because the wife is driving the car from her side. If she dares to say anything, she is often met with a verbal lashing, a tirade, and angry grunts from her husband. It can be common for the car to be filled with stress and tension. Typically, the wife (or mother) in this case gets blamed for causing the ruckus. Often, this blame is because her conduct seems the most noticeable and responsible for the difficulty. Men will say things like "Why do you always do that? I am a safe driver." Then, the man touts his safe driving record and quotes statistics about how safe he is. She is not typically appeased, and she will likely continue to cling to the handle on her side.

Is there another way to look at front-seat drivers and their responses? Instead of making fun of them, perhaps we can try to see their unique perspective. I believe the answer to problems arising from front-seat driving is not in getting the passenger to stop, but in getting the driver to have empathy and understanding. When the husband knows and understands what it feels like for the wife to be in the passenger seat with him driving, things really can begin to change.

In my family, I have typically been the front-seat driver. Because I have had to drive for work so much, I often find myself letting my wife drive when we go somewhere together. At these times, I have almost always engaged in all of the earlier mentioned front-seat driving techniques. Each time, I received the typical, tense and defensive response. I was stressed. My wife was stressed. Conflict often erupted between us as I held the dashboard, made commentary, or pleaded for her to slow down (while stomping the floor on my side!). It became kind of a stressful time for us. I wanted her to drive, but she was afraid of my response. We ended up hating going places in the car. It seemed it was all my fault, but I did not know what to do. I could not stop myself.

Then, the idea hit me. I had never told my wife what my experience was like sitting on this side of the car. I asked her whether she would please listen and try to understand what I might be experiencing from my side of the street. I told her I was in no way trying to find fault with her or her driving; I just wanted her to understand me and my feelings and experience. So I told her what it was like when my mother and I were hit by a semi-truck and knocked over seventy-five feet. I told her how I felt when I was out of control in the vehicle because of that experience. I reminded her (trying to be extra-sensitive) about the time I was riding in the passenger seat when she crashed into the cars in front of us. I told her of the fear I felt and the stress it caused me when I felt we were out of control. I even said I did not fully understand all the reasons I became so anxious, but it happened. I kindly told her that I did not like to feel this way. I expressed appreciation for her being the driver, and I asked her kindly for her help. She responded with empathy and compassion. I felt heard and understood. The real test was what happened when we got in the car next. It was better. Not perfect (because perfection is just not reality!), but it got better. I was grateful.

Many of life's challenges can be solved through understanding and empathy. When we seek to communicate and listen with respect and fully trying to understand, most things can resolve on their own. Often, in things like front-seat driving, we are just engaged in misunderstanding and confusion. This misunderstanding can provoke defensiveness and even contempt. When we slow down (literally and metaphorically) and really listen, seek to understand, and respond with compassion and love, things often change quickly. There is great value in seeing things from another's point of view. We all need to sit in someone else's seat every once in awhile.

So if someone is pounding the floor next to you, clinging to the chicken handles, and gasping out dynamic verbosity, instead of being impatient and insensitive with the person, perhaps you can try to listen and really "get it." Then, when you are sure you have understood, try to make some adjustments because you care. If you are the foot-stomping, white-knuckler, perhaps you can do as I did and find a quiet time to share your experience in a loving way. Great things can happen when we have empathy and understanding.

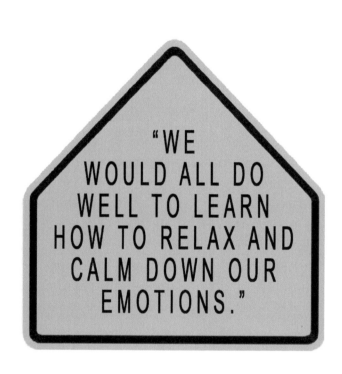

Chapter 13

Handling Road Rage

It has been said you can tell a lot about a person by how he or she responds to the minor irritations in life. I think it should be a required part of dating and premarital classes for everyone to ride in the car with his or her partner during a terrible traffic jam. This would be an ideal time to find out what your loved one is really like. You could even arrange it on your own sometime. Plan a date and purposely have your partner drive. Then, take her right into a rush-hour or construction zone. Sit back and observe what happens to her mood and behavior. It may help you to assess how she does at other things.

Though I have not always been free from this behavior, I find I really struggle to understand road rage in most cases. I remember once driving in a work truck to a meeting on the other side of town. I was on the freeway and moving about five miles per hour more than the posted speed limits. I was in the left-hand lane and was blocked in by cars in the middle lane. Another truck came racing up behind me and began to ride on my tail. I thought it was obvious I was unable to move over and let him pass (which I would normally do). I did not wish to drive any faster because it was an older truck, a company truck, and I did not like to speed. So I watched him continue to ride my bumper until I had an opportunity to change lanes and let him get by. The opening finally came and I started to get over. But before I could, he swerved into the middle lane before I did and gunned it past me. This behavior was not expected, but I was not too concerned about it. He would surely not be the first (or the last) person to do this. I thought he would just go on to wherever he needed to be in such a hurry. He did not.

My bumper-loving friend pulled in front of me and quickly hit his brakes. He then drove slowly in the left-hand lane. He continued to slow to almost a snail's pace. When I tried to get over to the middle lane, he stayed with me and kept us both going at this very slow pace. I admit my heart was racing a little because I did not know what he was going to do. However, I determined I would keep going as long as he was going. So I don't know for how long we played this little game, but I just patiently drove, making sure he did not do anything to make me hit him or something. I did not make any eye-contact with him in the mirror, nor did I do anything even to acknowledge his actions. I merely drove carefully behind him at less than thirty miles an hour in the fast lane. Then, apparently tired of this activity, he turned completely around in the driver's seat, stuck his head out of the small window, and said nice and kind words to me while politely waving his middle finger. He did this for the longest distance. (Yes! He was now not even watching the road in front of him.) Again, when I did not respond, he must have grown weary because he turned around and took off at a very high speed. Fortunately, I never saw him again, and I was grateful nothing more happened. Yet I still cannot forget what he did and how he acted. What is it that causes us to act like this in such situations? Truly, this man's behavior made absolutely no sense. Also, it clearly did not get him any closer to his own destination that day.

The answer is really quite simple: This man who wanted to give a kiss to both bumpers of my truck was hijacked—emotionally hijacked. In a moment of frustration, he, like all of us can be, was unable to see what he was doing and how nonsensical it was. He was not only being unsafe, but he was also being irrational and irresponsible. He was not progressing in his own journey because he seemingly had to spend a few more moments with me. What did he accomplish in this endeavor (beside getting a chapter in my book!)?

I remember learning about emotions in school. One of the most profound principles I ever learned had to do with emotional hijackings like this one. When I teach this principle to others, I draw four arrows. The first one is pointing up. It is labeled "Emotions." When our emotions go up, three things go down. I will then draw three arrows pointing down. The second arrow is labeled "rational thought." The third is "self-confidence," and the fourth is "self-efficacy." I will take some time to illustrate what these arrows mean and how they might affect us.

First, when our emotions get too high, we are likely to stop thinking clearly. Think about it! When have you ever said or done something you regretted? I would bet, like most of us, it was at a time of emotional excess. Your elevated emotions hijacked your brain and you literally found yourself doing or saying something you normally would not. This situation is even true with positive emotions. Too much emotion of any kind can create this hijacking effect. Then, if not checked, we begin to experience the next consequence.

If the emotion continues to be too intense for any period of time, individuals often begin to feel a lack of self-confidence and liking for oneself. You see this a lot in people who are depressed and frustrated. Verbally, they might give voice to their thoughts in phrases like "I am so stupid!" and "I mess everything up!" People who are experiencing emotions at the hijacking level are often guilty of also turning on themselves. In those moments, they may be even more prone to doing something dumb. If you are not thinking clearly and you don't really feel a lot of self-love, it makes sense you might do something you are not going to be proud of later.

Then, this whole notion of self-efficacy comes into play. When the rational thought is gone and self-confidence has plummeted, we often begin to experience a decrease in feelings of self-efficacy. What is self-efficacy? It is the belief that I have the resources, talents, and skills to solve this problem. In short, it is believing I am able and capable as a person. If too upset or too emotional for too long, we risk losing our self-confidence and our sense of capability. This is not a good state to be in.

So much of road rage and other losses of temper can be attributed to this interplay of emotions, rational thought, and feelings about ourselves and our skills and resources. Usually, after we have calmed down, we sit back and wonder what happened. Sometimes, we are in utter disbelief that we just did or said what we just did. Frequently, we try to apologize, saying things which are true like, "I was not in my right mind." Then, we wish we had not done such despicable things. Filled with regret, we wonder how this process happened. The answer is as simple as having allowed too much emotion to lead to all these other factors.

We would all do well to learn how to relax and calm down our emotions. We don't hear much about it anymore, but the old practice of counting to 100 when you are upset (or too emotional) is a wonderful practice. When the breathing slows, the heart rate declines, and the head clears, we are better prepared to handle what life delivers to us. When calm, we are less likely to do dumb stuff like chase someone down the road, or rant and rave in front of him. We save embarrassment, hassle, and even accident and injury when we focus on keeping ourselves composed and rational. It is a worthwhile skill to learn.

Chapter 14

Armed and NOT Dangerous

I have a gun I carry in my car. It is not licensed and I don't have a permit to have it with me. Yet I take it with me whenever I go anywhere in my car. This gun is special to me and I have had it my entire life. Of course, I did not know how to use it as an infant, but I was quickly taught and became skilled with it. I never go anywhere without my gun. It is not a real metal gun with bullets; it's just made up of my index finger and my thumb, so I can shape my hand quickly into my precious gun. I use this gun often when driving down the road. It is one of the best features that I always want in any car I drive.

I used to struggle with feelings of irritation, anger, and even some rage when I would encounter crazy drivers on the road. I have been guilty of tailgating someone who cut me off in traffic or turned in front of me and made me slow down. I have honked, made angry faces, and waved my arms in frustration at others. I have never made the one-finger gesture as I could never get myself to be that rude, but I have pretty much excused all of my other actions. There have surely been times when I have been out of control. However, these times did not last very long. I did not like how I felt and how those feelings affected me later. In short, I do not like to lose control of my emotions. I have never liked it when I am around other people who erupt in rage at the drop of a hat, so I am resolved not to do the same. Though I have slipped, I have made road rage disappear from my life. I did it by arming myself with my little gun. This is why I have it with me whenever I drive anywhere. It is essential.

Emotions can be difficult to control. Sometimes when I am upset enough to get hijacked by them, I need something to help me relax even more than just breathing or counting to 100. This is when my little road gun comes in handy. Combined with a couple of other strategies, I can discharge my "handgun" and stop any and all road rage. It works by first understanding how our thoughts and feelings are connected. Emotions, like anger and rage, are always preceded by a thought. Typically, the thought triggers the emotions and a behavioral response can quickly follow. You cannot feel emotions without thinking something (even thoughts seemingly below our awareness produce our feelings). This knowledge is powerful because it can help us change our feelings and have greater self-control.

Even more, there is a strategy I have come to call "thought replacement." It is simple: When you are bothered by a thought you do not want to have, you simply replace it with another thought. Then, for greater impact, you engage yourself in a simple physical action to reinforce the change in thoughts. The pairing of a replacement-thought with a different physical activity can help you to change emotional directions—often quite quickly. You may wonder about the physical action and how it relates, but you have probably experienced this situation over and over again. Have you ever walked from one room of your home to another and completely forgotten why you went to that room? Then maybe you went back to the first room and immediately recalled the reason for your actions. If you have experienced this, you have seen firsthand the power of thinking and movement. You forgot because you were moving. There is personal power in this knowledge. Power that has helped me to eliminate road rage entirely from my life.

Here is what I do. My replacement thought is "Boom!" I will even say it out loud (usually when no one else is in the car). Then, I fire my gun at the offending car and driver. It did not work the very first time I tried it. Yet after many pairings of this verbal-thought "Boom" and the firing of my gun, I no longer feel any swellings of negative emotions inside me. They actually seem just to melt away. In fact, I often find myself firing my gun and thinking "Boom!" before I am even aware of the emotions. It has become an automatic replacement behavior, sparing me a lot of frustration on the road. I admit it has also earned me some silly looks from my wife, kids, and their friends in the car. However, I am 100 percent road rage free. I like it!

Perhaps when you find yourself upset by events, circumstances, or situations (like being cut off or irritated by crazy drivers), you can try this thought-replacement technique. Pair a new thought with a simple physical activity. Over time, you will find yourself developing a new response habit. It is powerful. It can really help. Feel free to use the gun! Together, we may be the only armed and NOT dangerous people on the road!

Chapter 15

Learning the Lessons of Parallel Parking

I hear it from just about every driver I know: "I hate parallel parking!" I have friends and family members who will park miles away and walk rather than parallel park right in front of their destination. I know people who get so stressed about parallel parking that they can barely function. Panic sets in and there is no remedy available. I am guessing this experience must be more general to most people. Many of my friends are excited that cars are now being developed that can actually handle this task for you. I am not really sure how they work, but from the commercials I've seen, it appears all you do is line up right and push a button and the car parks itself. Wow! Incredible stuff!

I am proud to say I love parallel parking. In driver's education class in high school, it was my very best subject. I grasped the idea quickly, implemented it, and became (in my humble opinion) quite good at it. Parallel parking may be one of only a few subjects where I am good at something everyone else is not good at. I am enjoying this moment. I love being able to say I am skilled in at least one thing!

I personally believe everyone can be proficient and even an

expert at parallel parking. Now, since I am good at this (and my driver's ed. grades testify to the fact), I believe I am qualified to teach everyone how to be good at it. Right? I am an expert so this gives me license to speak on this topic. Actually, I am just going to take this chance to do so. If I am wrong, sorry! If not, try it. Go park!

As I have observed family members, friends, and even strangers in the process of parallel parking, I have seen a couple of common things. First, with a few exceptions, most of the people I have observed actually know how to parallel park. This means the person possesses the skill and knows the technique. Very rarely do I see someone clearly doing it wrong. So the problem for most people must not be in not knowing what to do. It must be something else.

The second thing I have observed in people pulling in to parallel park is how fast they go about the maneuver. Most try to go too fast. They zip up next to the car in front of where they wish to park and slam the car in reverse. Then, they try to pull into the spot as if they are at the Indy 500 and are fighting for pole position. Usually, this urgency results in frustration and a lack of success. Now, in frustration, the driver proceeds to do an inch back and forth kind of thing until he may be in the spot. I have seen some people then lean out the window, open the door, and even get out of the car and walk around it to see how they did. When they realize they somehow magically arranged the car in a more perpendicular than parallel direction, the red face and under-the-breath curses come out. The driver may even kick the tire at this point. It is no good! I have seen some get back in and try again by both pulling all the way out and then making a second qualifying-time run at it. Others will continue to do the inchworm thing, working to get the car in place. This whole process takes too long and causes great stress, so after this kind of trial, many would just prefer to avoid the experience altogether.

The key to success in parallel parking and so many other aspects of life is in going slowly. If the driver will just slow down, perform the task with precision, and move forward with confidence and patience, he or she will succeed. Being patient and slow is what I am good at! I will pull up to the car in front of the spot. Then, I will carefully pull back until at the pivot point where I begin to turn the wheel. Carefully and still slowly, I reverse myself into the spot, often just the right distance from the curb. It works when you are willing to take it slowly.

Most of the skills and attributes we need to possess in life are acquired in the same way. The old saying is "Things that grow slowly live longer." This statement is true in learning anything and becoming skilled at it; for example, you work slowly at learning to play an instrument, learning a computer skill, or developing a new habit. The brain is really amazing. When you are willing to do something slowly and correctly the first time, you increase your likelihood of success. If you continue to practice slowly and with exactness, you further embed the process in your brain. Once the process is ingrained, it can be accelerated. Be careful not to speed up too fast, but gradually pick up the pace. Over time and through repetition, the carefully initiated and integrated process becomes almost automatic and unconscious. Carefully entered data and processes can sometimes be accelerated to any speed necessary. Sometimes the accuracy and safety required means you will always choose to do it slowly. Many of us are just too impatient to take it slowly.

We live in a world that emphasizes instant messaging, instant oatmeal, and immediate gratification. We have fast cars to take us to get fast food. We want everything now and we resent anything that makes us have to slow down and wait. We are trained to see everything in terms of how quickly it can be accomplished rather than the rewards of accuracy and precision. We want what we want; we insist on having it now; and we will continue to fight at high speeds even when we are unsuccessful. Sometimes in our rash and hasty pace, we make significant errors and fail even more. What was supposed to be parallel becomes perpendicular because we are not willing to slow down and do it right the first time. Some things need to be done quickly. Yet there is wisdom in knowing when to slow down and do it well and properly.

I have seen the commercials of the smart car careening around the corner, racing on the street near the apartment and hectically sliding into the perfect parallel park. I suppose that works for stunt drivers. Honestly, I am guessing those drivers did as I suggest here—they probably practiced over and over again at slower speeds until they could do it perfectly. Personally, since I don't have an unlimited supply of takes and cars, I just take it slowly the first time and get it right. A lot of good can result when we take it slowly and do it right. If you need to speed up, you can. However, don't be afraid to take it slow. You are probably better skilled and capable than you believe. Maybe you should slow down and see!

"WHEN WE ARE OKAY WITH THE
SPECIAL CHARACTERISTICS
MAKING EACH OF US
HIS OR HER OWN
PERSON,
WE CAN REALLY
FIND JOY AND
VIBRANCY
IN LIFE."

Chapter 16

Thinking of Others

I believe I am like most other drivers on the road. I believe in carpooling to conserve fuel and money and take care of the environment by creating less air pollution. Yet most days of the week, you will find me alone in my car. Yes. Almost always, I am the only person in my car, driving alone to work. As I look around, I can see I am not alone in being alone. Most of the cars around me only have a solitary person heading to a destination. Let's face it; most of us spend a lot of time alone in the car.

Being alone in the car is an interesting experience. You are in control of everything. You get to choose the radio station. Or, if you want, you can plug in your iPod and jam out. You have full reign over the temperature, the volume, the window height, the reclining position of the seat, and more. If you drive alone often, you can put things where you want them and leave them there. Being alone is powerful. You are the king or queen of this moving castle. Whatever happens there is in your ultimate power! You rule this little mobile world. I love my little dominion! It is mine! All mine! (Insert evil and controlling laugh!)

I can tell that my car is my domain and I want to own it and control it because every time my wife or children want to borrow my car, I get a little uptight. My wife likes to sit farther back and stretch her long legs out. She is shorter than me, but she still moves my seat farther back. My daughter is taller than her mom, but she loves to be up extra close to the steering wheel and the dashboard. Obviously, my radio stations are not good enough for my daughter since she could not possibly stand any kind of news or talk radio. So she has to pick the station with the loudest bass sounds and crank it up. Often, she will adjust all the sound settings too. She has to have it just right. My wife will pop in some book on CD and leave it in. So I will get in and be blasted with some narrator right in the middle of a compelling scene, and I have no idea what is happening. I sometimes want to listen, but I have already missed the storyline. Even more, my family does not always respect this pristine environment that is mine. I like to keep my car organized and clean. But after my family members use it, I may find candy wrappers, fast-food outlet bags, and more. My little royal sanctuary often gets desecrated by the insensitive lower folk. How can they be so disrespectful of my space? I feel violated.

Of course, like other drivers who share their cars, I know about all these things because I discover them when I get in to drive to work. I could be blasted by the radio or the heater on full blast. I might have to turn down the volume, the temperature, or the mirror. I know who drove before me by how close my knees are to my mouth. If I am swallowing them whole and almost gagging, it was my daughter. If I have my legs almost straight, it was my wife. Then, the effect is magnified because she has leaned back the seat. Sometimes I look to see whether there might be a pair of dice on the mirror when I am reclined way back, the stereo is thumping, and I can barely see out the window. Looking around, I feel the need to make numerous adjustments. It almost seems like the previous driver spun in a Tasmanian-Devil-like circle, changing every setting, moving every knob, and adjusting anything that can move. Then, because it is my car, it takes me considerable effort to get everything back in place. It has to be just right. Do you know how hard it is to move the seat with that weird metal bar thing and get it just right? Frustratingly, I will have adjusted the mirrors before the seat and then have to fix them all again. It is agonizing! How could my loved ones do this to me and my precious little car?

Well, here is a little truth I have learned. They may be doing something to my car, but they are most certainly not doing anything to me. They are simply adjusting everything to their needs and preferences. In many cases, the changes represent things I would want them to do in my car. For instance, I want my daughter close enough to the pedals and the steering wheel so she can be safe. If I stop to think about it, I really want this adjustment, albeit inconvenient for me, so she can be as safe as possible. Same for my wife. Even more, I really want my family to be happy. I love it when my wife and children are smiling and laughing and enjoying life. It is one of the greatest sources of joy in my life. There is nothing more important to me than their happiness and well-being. Or at least, there should not be anything more important.

So I am rethinking this whole mobile-castle-and-I-am-supreme-ruler thing. If I truly want my wife and children to be happy, then, perhaps I need to think more about them when they borrow my car. If I am thinking of them and their happiness and safety first, I could perhaps be grateful when I have to make adjustments when I get in the car. If I am thinking of others, I can be more sensitive to their needs.

As we travel through life, how important is it that we are sensitive to our fellow travelers? Each of us is different in so many ways with varied interests, unusual quirks, and specific needs and desires. Does it seem strange to have to move things around a little to make them work? Not everyone can be what I would wish him or her to be. Even more, I would not want anyone to expect me to be just like him. I like being unique or special in my own ways. Perhaps, if I am more sensitive to other people, they will in turn be more sensitive to me. If I can recognize what talents, interests, and gifts they bring to the driver's seat, I will likely be more caring and compassionate. If I see their unique contribution as valuable and their differences from me as exciting, it makes it easier to be grateful for them. Also, it is easier for me to adapt when things need to be put back in place for my own individual preferences. It seems when we are okay with the special characteristics making each of us his or her own person, we can really find joy and vibrancy in life.

So I am resolved to do a couple of things here. I find benefit in thinking of others and what they bring to this world, making it more special and beautiful. I am striving to let go of the little things that could frustrate me as I share this world with others. Finally, I am trying to be more sensitive when I sit in their seats. I want to be more caring and understanding in my seat and when I find myself in theirs.

I just pulled into the garage in my wife's van. I think I will turn the radio back to her favorite station, turn off the heat, and move the seat back a little. She probably won't even notice, but I can imagine how happy she will be. And I'll know I made her happy by thinking of her first!

Chapter 17

Don't Honk Unless
You Have to Honk

Whenever my family has purchased a car new to us, the kids are always so excited to get in it and climb all over the seats and such. Then they want to know what the horn sounds like. This curiosity would not bother me so much if we were not always in the garage at the time. They hit the horn and it echoes and hurts your ears. Then, they have to do it again. Then, each of the kids has to do it. Then, because one of them pushed it fifteen times, the others have to push it fifteen times in order for it to be fair. If you have kids, you know this scenario. Sometimes I think the reason why older people cannot hear is because they have had to listen as all their kids have honked the horn the same number of times. Kids love the horn. Some adults do too!

Somewhere along the way, I grew out of love with honking a car horn. As a young driver, I used to pound the horn at just about every turn. It was a way to greet friends, get them to come out of the house so we can go, and let your date's father know how cool you were. (This one never seemed to work, though adolescent boys insist on doing it!) The horn also was an important form of emotional expression. Many of us may remember the onslaught of "Honk if you love..." bumper stickers. Occasionally, you will still spot people on the curb holding up signs saying "Honk to support...!" Even more, honking was a way to communicate love and caring as you said goodbye and waved one last time. Finally, the horn seems to be a primary means of communicating displeasure over other people's driving. You can honk before you wave with one finger at a driver who cut you off! You can honk and shout, "Hey!" and throw both hands in the air. Some people's horn-honking behavior is accompanied by an equal amount of honking noises from their mouths. There are many ways to use a car horn.

Have you ever wondered what the horn was really created for in the first place? It almost always emits a rather harsh and unpleasant sound. I know this is true because my wife has always hated it when I see how high she can jump when I push it while she is right in front of the car. Not many of us are happy with the sounds of our car horns. We most certainly cannot all be driving the General Lee from *The Dukes of Hazzard* while some catchy tune plays. Very few of us will ever own a car with tunes playing like you are heading through town as part of the local parade. With few exceptions, horns were programmed to be unpleasant, abrasive, and intolerable to the ear. They were made to get our attention, wake us up, and perhaps move us to action. They are hard on the ears.

Just recently, the horn on my old car broke and started honking every time I used the left turn signal. Then it started just honking indiscriminately and getting stuck. The only way to stop the dreadful noise was to pound the center of the steering wheel with all my might. When this solution finally stopped working or my fist hurt too much from punching the car repeatedly, I had to remove the fuses to get it to stop. Believe me, you will not like your car horn when it blares uncontrollably and repeatedly. Your ears will ring, your temples will be pounding, and you will have odd flashbacks of scary '80s boy bands. It will be a terrible experience! Horns are just not meant to be used or heard that much.

I have come to see my car horn as having a very select and distinct purpose. I believe the car horn was primarily invented to help keep me and my passengers safe from injury and accident as much as possible. When I started to view my horn in this way, it changed the frequency and reasoning behind its use. Now, I rarely use the horn. If I can tell there is imminent danger or a possible collision, I will gladly honk the horn. If I can tell someone may be hurt if another is not alerted to the danger of his current actions or inactions, I will give the horn a push. In applying the horn, I will only press it enough to secure the desired result. Then, I move on. When the horn became for me a precise, event-specific tool used for creating safety, I found I rarely needed to use it.

You see, as a human, I can choose to communicate in more effective ways in all other arenas. I have my voice to communicate love and pleasure and support. I can exercise gentlemanly manners and respect by getting out of the car and going to the door to get my date. I can support causes I really love by purchasing their products, donating to their fund-raisers, or volunteering my time to support them. I can more kindly express my disappointments and frustrations in soft tones and respectful phrasing. Even better, I can let all the little things that bug me too much slide off and pay them less heed. I can express love, playful teasing, excitement, support, and much more without the horn. I rarely need it for any of my communication needs. I need it when there is danger, but that is all I really need it for.

It would be well if we learned to stop any unnecessary honking we may be doing. There are so many better ways to relay our messages. When we honk too loudly, too harshly, and too often, we so often fail to get the desired response. If we honk too much at our spouses, they may feel hurt, wounded, angry, defensive, or afraid. They may begin to honk back, causing us to experience some of the same reactions. If we honk too much at our kids, they may shut down, retreat inside, and be damaged emotionally. They also may start honking back. Sometimes those we honk at too much go to other places and honk at the people there. As a result, we have teachers honking at students, bosses honking at their employees, and bullies honking at little kids on the playground. With all this honking going on, people begin to feel hurt, anxious, defensive, and on guard. Soon everyone is jumpy and on edge, quick to honk, and slow to listen. Eventually, no one is listening because no one is really talking. Nobody wants to listen to the harsh sounds of honking.

I believe the horn on my car is a valuable thing. I definitely want it. However, I choose to honk only when absolutely necessary. When the horn is not required, I try to think of the myriad of other ways I can more effectively get my message across. Things go so much better this way. Don't honk if you love this message. Perhaps, you can just nod and smile and share this chapter with someone you love. That is something really worth doing!

"ANYTIME WE SEEK TO CUT OTHER PEOPLE OFF, WE CAN **CREATE AN ACCIDENT** THAT MAY INJURE THEM AND WILL SURELY HURT US."

Chapter 18

Causing the Accident

I feel absolutely awful when I think about the day I caused a car accident. I was being selfish and stupid, and because of my choices and actions, other people got into a wreck. I was not cited, no one blamed me, and I was not involved, but I caused the accident because I was only thinking of myself.

I was headed home on a clear summer day. I was on a nice four-lane road driving the speed limit. I was in the left-hand lane about a mile or so away from my turn-off. A car full of what appeared to be teenage girls came up beside me on the right. I noticed them because they were going very fast and seemed to be acting pretty wild. There was a car in front of them in their lane going slower than the speed limit. When the teenage female driver sped up, I guessed she was going to try to swerve in front of me and pass us all. At that moment, two very significant events happened simultaneously. One of them, I will regret—maybe forever.

The driver in front of the girls stepped on his brakes and, at the same time, put on his right-hand turn signal to turn into the small strip mall there. My choice? I chose to speed up at the exact same moment. I am not really sure what I was thinking, but I guess I thought I would keep the girls from cutting me off. Well, I succeeded. I remember the driver's face as she looked over her left shoulder to see whether she could zip in front of me as she planned. Seeing I was closer than she thought I was, she turned her vehicle to stay in her lane. Unfortunately, because she had stepped on the gas to race in front of me, she was clearly unable to stop in time for the car trying to turn right. The sound of her car smashing into the other car and the screaming of girls was terrible. There was no squealing of tires because she did not even have enough time to hit her brakes. She hit him while accelerating. It was terrible to watch. In the eyes of the law, it was her fault. But I knew it was really my fault. I stopped to make sure everyone was okay (probably to assuage my own guilt). The driver in the front car was shaken but okay. I cannot believe what I did after I made sure he was okay. I said, "I saw what happened" and gave him my contact information. I could not get myself to go and talk to the girls, but they all appeared uninjured. I drove away feeling ashamed of myself. I could not believe what I had just caused.

How often do we find ourselves in this same situation, both on the road and in life? I am certain I am not the only person who has ever sped up to keep someone from getting in front of him. People have done it to me so many times. I see it happen to others. I have been in many a car where the driver did exactly what I was doing that day. It seems like innocent behavior. I am guessing that most of the time no accident happens, and we are left with irritated people or people feeling some kind of vindication or smug, but empty satisfaction. Why do we get pleasure in keeping someone from doing what he wants to do? Most of the time, we don't even know the people, but we get some odd pleasure out of keeping them from cutting us off. Again, most of these moments pass without incident. But what about those feelings?

I am persuaded that something very wrong is happening in these moments on the road. Aside from the obvious potential for accidents and injury coming to us and others, I believe we are causing personal harm to ourselves. When we seek to dominate, control, or otherwise force or manipulate other people, we create harm. Sometimes we harm others (as my accident did). Always, we hurt ourselves. We simply cannot control or force others to do things they do not wish to do. When we try to impose our will upon others, it creates a sense of power and control inside us that can grow and create dark and ugly feelings.

One of the most powerful attributes people seem to possess is will. Most people come into this world with a sense of independence that can be quite powerful. We start to notice when a child learns to say "No." Then, we see it in the child's behavior. Have you ever tried to take things away from young children? They have some impressive evasive maneuvers. It can be baffling to a much older and larger adult to be defied by a little child. I remember hearing the stories of my brother as a baby getting a handful of spaghetti. He dodged every attempt to get it from him and splattered everything within about a ten-foot radius. Later, when kids get older, they move from physical means to more cognitive means. The approaches become more sophisticated. All of this is an expression of will.

All too often, parents, teachers, spouses, and others respond to these expressions of will with displays of control or domination. They will try to manpower others into doing what they desire or wish. In short, they seek to cut them off. A larger, stronger person may temporarily be able to control someone smaller and weaker. However, there is a part in all people that cannot be controlled or mastered. Most parents come to realize previous controlling actions end up not working later on. Often, controlling spouses come to the same conclusion. None of us wants to be forced to do anything. It is just against our natural will.

I attempted to control what an adolescent girl driver was doing on the road one day. In this case, it caused a bad accident. I was wrong. My response and the consequence of my choice were immediately harmful to her and others around her. I could witness what my controlling actions caused right in front of me. It will not always be so clear when we seek to dominate a family member or friend through emotional, physical, or mental means. Worse, the action harmed me. I first engaged in justification for my behavior, which permitted me to take actions to hide my accountability and pretend I did nothing wrong or harmful. This kind of justification, if left unchecked, could cause irreparable harm to my feelings of self-worth and lead to future unkind behavior. Justification is classic in domestic abusers and those who engage in violence and control. They are great at justifying why they had to do what they did. I also left the scene with feelings of guilt and shame for my conduct. I felt badly that my choice caused harm to other people. Even if the girl was partly at fault, the passengers and the other driver were surely not. I made a choice resulting in harm coming to innocent people.

Feelings of guilt and shame can blossom into a whole variety of ailments for an individual. Most addictions and many other social and emotional challenges have their roots in these feelings. It was not just a simple thing happening that day. I caused an accident and most definitely did not walk away unharmed. Anytime we seek to cut other people off, we can create an accident that may injure them and will surely hurt us.

Chapter 19

Letting People In

Have you ever been driving on a nice two-lane road that merges into one lane? You are plugging along in your lane doing fine, but now you have to share your space with all the people in the other lane. Have you noticed what this activity creates in other people? It can be interesting, instructive, and even scary to witness what happens to people in these moments.

In my neighborhood, there is a main road many take to head toward the freeway. The right lane of this road merges into the left just before you enter the freeway. Every morning, the left lane is completely backed up with people slowly moving forward. The right lane appears to be shorter at first, but then it becomes all backed up just a little farther down the road. When I take this road, I choose just to get in the left lane because I know it is the lane I need to be in. It may seem to take longer, but it is where I need to be. Others, however, will zip into the right lane and seek to get over wherever they can. You know what often comes next. People in the left lane begin to become concerned about those in the right lane. Some will speed up until they are almost touching the bumper of the car in front of them. They are saying, "No way are you getting in front of me, pal!" They will maintain this close distance until they make it impossible for vehicles in the right lane to merge in. Still others will go to even greater lengths. They will move their cars to the right, straddling the line and blocking the right lane. This seems to say, "I own this road! I had to wait in this long line, so you will too!" I cannot speak for everyone, but this whole scenario just creates too much anxiety in me. So I take another route to work.

To me, it seems that individual thinking, territory grabbing, and progress-blocking activities seem to slow the whole group down. If my thinking is correct, if the whole group is slowed, then each individual is going to be slowed also. I have never done a rigorous scientific study on this, but it seems to me there is a better way.

The answer is so simple I fear most will not believe it will really result in forward progress. I believe the best answer is to let others in. Simply put, when a car comes to merge into your lane, let it in. If everyone does this, you can get a really cool looking alternating pattern. I have wondered whether it looks like a braid from the sky when everyone does this. More importantly, by letting people in, it seems to make things so much smoother. I notice in those moments that even if it does not make me go forward faster, it feels like it! I feel better when I let people in.

Some of you are thinking right now, "But what about the yahoo who purposely chose the right lane and is trying to race in front of all of us who are patiently choosing the left lane?" We have all seen these yahoos. It can be very frustrating when this happens. Yet I believe that if you had an attitude of "Let them in," you could handle it better. If you focus more on what you are doing and what your plan and attitude is, then you are focused on something you can control. When we concentrate on our response and choice, we make better choices.

You see, it is too easy to jump to conclusions and confusions when you begin to think too much about what other people are doing. In cases such as these merge examples, I am guessing few of us have actually thought, "Oh, that poor driver must have not known the right lane ended here!" I am guessing our inner workings are much more negative and judgmental in these moments. Let's face it! It is really easy to sit on our little throne and pronounce judgments on other drivers. It is easy to assume the worst about them, and then, in that state, stop thinking. This mindset leads to a focus on individuals instead of progress. We zero in on what we think someone else is trying to do, judge it, and slow the progress of all of us. The simple solution is to let others in. Yes! Regardless of the reasons why they are needing to merge, please just let them in.

Life becomes so much easier for all of us when we let people in. When we think about the welfare of all of us as a group, we will want to let people in. When we think about all of our progress and sincerely want all of us to progress, we will want to let people in. We cannot control all the reasons or really any of the reasons why people do what they do, but we can be resolved to let them in, to include them, to encourage them with a wave to come on over, to cheer them on and bring them into our lane. Allow them in. It changes you. It changes them. It helps us all move a little better down the road. And, if it is not really faster, it sure feels better.

To be sure, each one of us will someday find ourselves in a lane ending with a merge. In those moments, we will look over our shoulders and wish to be let in. We will hope to find a caring individual who motions for us to come on over. In those moments, we will likely wave, mouth a "Thank you," and smile. We will be grateful. It is just a better way to do things. We all feel better when someone lets us in, so let us do the same for others.

"LIFE BECOMES SO MUCH EASIER FOR ALL OF US WHEN WE LET PEOPLE IN."

Chapter 20

Using Your Turn Signal

$\mathbf{A}$ while back, I was pulling out of the gas station and heading the rest of the way to work. The turn out of this station is kind of wide and put me quickly at the intersection and ready to turn left. I tried to turn on the left-hand turn signal, but because of the angle of the wheel, I could not do it. It has the auto-shut off mechanism, which when the wheel is turned as it was, will not work. So I waited to turn left until it was clear. The driver across the intersection was clearly not pleased with me since he was waiting to turn left as well. When I did not go forward as he expected me to do, he squealed in front of me, waved at me with one finger, and yelled obscenities at me. I felt terrible inside, and at first, I did not understand why he was so upset. Then, when it hit me, I felt unfairly judged. I had tried to use my signal, but my car would not let me. I was shaken inside at his outburst, but I could understand his feelings—too many people do not use their turn signals anymore. It can be very frustrating.

Turn signals are really a great idea. I can signal my intentions on the road so other drivers know what I plan to do. If I intend to change lanes, I can make it known with the flip of a little switch. If I plan to turn at the corner, I can also advise others. Likewise, they can let me know what their plan for their drive is. Such a little device is so very helpful. I believe in using my turn signals every time I drive. Surely, I have missed a time or two using them, but I find them very helpful. There are even times when I will signal way in advance to make sure everyone knows what I am going to do. For instance, there is this busy road on my way to work where traffic moves really fast. I have found it wise to signal my intention to turn well ahead of the actual corner. Signaling gives the person behind me extra notice and sufficient time to slow down or change lanes before I slow down. I think this practice is helpful, keeps us all safe, and works to communicate in simple ways. I highly advocate the use of turn signals.

What are the turn signals we have to communicate in everyday life? Are there simple communication strategies we can employ as we navigate each day that are as useful as our car signals? I believe there are. I believe they can be simple words, gestures, and behaviors that make a difference in how we relate to each other and move through the roads of life. It can be just as important for you and me to go through each day signaling our intentions to others as it is to point which way you are going to take your car on your next commute. Most of these signals are simple and can help make things better.

I have found that many social interaction problems result from assumptions not being clearly communicated. Misunderstandings can occur frequently as we try to support each other and work together in various settings. We can jump to conclusions, become angry, and feel unloved and unsupported. Tempers flare at times when these moments happen. Just as the driver who thought I should be going straight got angry when I did something different, when we do not know what others are going to do, conditions may be ripe for friction and conflict. The practice of employing simple communication strategies can make the difference.

For me, most of these approaches are simple verbal gestures. I will often forecast what I am about to do with my family. For instance, I will check in with my wife about my plans for after work. I may tell her my intention to stop at the store, get gas for the car, and then be home a few minutes later than usual. As a parent, I will let my kids know I plan to leave in ten minutes, so if they want to go with me, they need to be ready. I will tell people I am behind them. I will broadcast I am carrying something heavy or hot. When assisting a child or someone with disabilities, I will likely tell the person exactly what I am going to do before I take any action at all. I may say, "Now I am going to help you with...." or "You will feel my hand on your back as I help you to...." It is not too difficult to declare my intentions.

The people I assist in resolving marital or family concerns find it so helpful to learn how to signal their interests, intentions, wishes, and desires. I find myself helping people to express their intentions and wishes to each other. It is not really hard (as easy as using a turn signal), but we do not always think to do it. When we work on signaling what we want, things often begin to happen. Signals can be as simple as stating an intention or desire. For example:

- I would really like to spend time with you this weekend.
- I was hoping we could talk about our plans.
- I was hoping to get to bed early tonight.
- I have been feeling a bit overwhelmed lately.

- I wish we did not have so much to do tonight.
- I am excited about the concert this weekend.

All of the above are examples of using our "turn signal" in relationships and interactions with others. We do a lot to help things move along smoother when we take the time to indicate where we are at, what we wish to do, and what we hope will happen. When others get this information, they are often much more responsive. A kindly expressed wish or preference can elicit supportive behavior, allow for adjustments, and facilitate more beneficial objectives. When we know, we can move in the right way.

If you are not in the habit of using a turn signal, I suggest you try it. Speak up about what you wish would happen. Tell someone what you were hoping to do. Communicate what you most want or feel. Give a clear indication of the "turn" you want to make. You will be surprised by how it helps "traffic" move along better.

"WE LIVE IN A SOCIETY THAT FOSTERS FAULT-FINDING AND POINTING OUT OTHERS' WEAKNESSES AND FRAILTIES. IT HAS BECOME ONE OF OUR FAVORITE PASTIMES TO INDULGE IN CRITICIZING AND CONDEMNING OTHERS."

Chapter 21

Slowly Going Around the World to the Right

There is this intersection by my house where I turn from one main road onto the highway. The angle of the turn is not sharp enough that when the wheel comes back, it turns off the turn signal. Almost every time I make this turn, I end up driving down the highway with my turn signal on. If my wife is in the car, she always catches it and tells me. My kids will sometimes notice and tell me. If no one is with me, I may not notice it for a long time. I hate it when I do that! I find it embarrassing. It is like forgetting to add the attachment to the email before you send it! No one likes to forget that! It is frustrating to forget these kinds of things. It is easy to get irritated with ourselves or with the person in front of us who has forgotten to click it off.

When I am behind someone who has neglected to turn off his blinker, I often find myself saying something a friend of mine always said, "Slowly going around the world to the right!" Then, I chuckle inside (and sometimes outside!) as I laugh about this fairly common human behavior. I am then able to acknowledge the common humanity of all of us and feel compassion for the person in front of me. Instead of my natural impulse to call him "stupid" or say something like "That goofball left his blinker on!" I find a different response. It is one of understanding.

It is so tempting to sit in the judgment seat when we see other people making mistakes. We sit in this comfortable place and pronounce some sort of statement about their obvious incapability and lack of intelligence. It is all too easy to point the finger at others and condemn them for the little things they do. We live in a society that fosters fault-finding and pointing out others' weaknesses and frailties. It has become one of our favorite pastimes to indulge in criticizing and condemning others.

It is interesting to me how much of what we criticize in others has roots in our own behavior. Much of what we may be irritated by when we see it in others is the same thing we see in ourselves—if we really choose to look for it. How can I make fun of or belittle someone with his turn signal still on when I am prone to do the same thing? How can I be angry when there is no attachment to my email when so often mine leave the outbox without required add-ons? It is so easy to find fault. It is much more difficult to have compassion and understanding.

That is why I like my friend's statement and say it to myself: "Slowly going around the world to the right." I like it because it reminds me how most of us have had this experience. In fact, if you go just about anywhere in the world where there are cars and turn signals, you will find people who have left them on. It is a common challenge. It happens to just about all of us. We all have times where we, like everyone else, are just going around in this world, imperfectly trying to navigate through. We make mistakes that are common to us all. I find power in acknowledging this. If I am doing something others routinely deal with, then I am not doing so badly. If others are doing something I have unintentionally done, then they are not doing so badly either. There is no place for judgment or self-righteousness when we take this position. How can I condemn anyone who merely does the same thing I find myself doing?

So the next time you see someone with his or her blinker still on, perhaps you can laugh at yourself and remember you do this too! When it is you with the blinker on, then you can remember that everywhere in this world people have done the same thing. It is our common humanity to leave blinkers on occasionally. So look in the mirror instead of a magnifying glass and forget about it. Laugh it off and keep slowly going around the world to the right!

Chapter 22

Stopping at All Lemonade Stands

When I was a child, it was a common thing for kids to set up a lemonade stand and try to sell a cool drink to people passing by. It was a fun project every time. It was exciting to make the sign, mix the lemonade, add too much sugar, and get everything out to the corner. Then came the initial fun of calling out to others, waving the sign, and smiling and beckoning to those who crossed our path. What a thrill when a customer came. I could clink the change in my little cup forever! I loved the sound! I felt lifted, buoyed by someone taking the time to support me! Some kids would even run in to tell their moms, "I just made a nickel, Mommy!" and race back to the stand. It was just pure summer fun! It was not so much about the money as about the experience. There is nothing like setting up a lemonade stand and doing a little fun business with the neighbors.

I am sad to say I cannot even remember the last time I saw little kids running a neighborhood lemonade stand. I wonder where they went. It was often a common thing to see cute little kids with homemade signs, pushing their homemade "brew" to anyone coming by. Now it seems like a rare occurrence. Where did all the lemonade stands go?

I won't pretend to have all the answers, but a couple of thoughts have crossed my mind. First, kids might not do this anymore because the response rate was never really that high. Even the best of sellers probably never generated much income off the lemonade stand venture. It is easy to be excited in the first few moments, but after the sun hits a peak and the heat comes, it seems easier to drink the profits and go play than engage in this pointless effort. Too often, the conclusion was it did not make enough money to make it worth it.

The other reason we may not see lemonade stands anymore may be more impactful and explains the loss even better. Kids are naturally eager to try things; they are infinitely more patient than most adults; they also love the reward and can often wait long times for it. So if this is the nature of kids, then why would lemonade stands disappear? I believe it is because not enough adults stopped. It is too easy to be preoccupied, in a hurry, and distracted to take the time to stop. Even more, we are often so rushed we don't even notice. Finally, it is not an easy thing to do. We have to stop what we are doing and take the time to visit with the children, offer them a kind word, sip the lemonade, and smile at them.

Life has changed in so many ways, but I believe we are missing something crucial here. The lemonade stand was never about the money. It was about a child being able to achieve something on his or her own and earning the love, praise, and recognition of others. It was about being validated by others. It was about the inner feeling of confidence that comes when your efforts produce a positive response. It is what I often call "a stamp in your passport of life," which says I am going someplace.

We seem to have lost this kind of encouragement and enthusiasm in our society. We have become so busy with all of our own pursuits that we may not even notice the person who needs a little encouragement, someone who will really listen, and a kind word of recognition for honest effort. We don't really listen when people ask us, "How are you today?" and we know they are not listening when they query us. We have people all around us offering up their own little lemonade stands of sorts, but we don't choose to see it. In the hustle to get here or there, we fail to see all the good we can do right in front of us. It is probably easier just to hand your kids the money or make them some lemonade. It is probably even simpler to give them a cell phone or tablet with games on it and let them go somewhere quiet so they won't disturb us. With adults in our life, it is probably easier to pass in the hallway with the cordial but empty greeting than it is to engage in meaningful interactions. It is easier to be quick to the things we need or want and miss the people behind them.

Rushing through life in this way probably gets us plenty of lemonade. Some of it will be sticky with too much sugar; some of it will be sour and make us squirm; some may be just perfect and bring back great memories and sensations. However, the real joy comes when we encourage the person who is selling the lemonade. When we stop what we are doing and really get connected with people, we really start to experience something joyful. We feel connected, we feel moved, and we feel changed. When we really see the people behind the lemonade stands, and we reach out and encourage them, life takes on new pleasures and meaning. It is the people we need to see. We don't stop at lemonade stands because we need lemonade. We stop because we need each other.

Chapter 23

Stopping to Help Others

I am so very grateful for the invention of cell phones. It is reassuring as a husband and father to know that if my wife and children were stranded when driving somewhere, they would have little difficulty getting in touch with me or connecting with someone to help. I remember back in the dark ages of telephone communication, being stuck on the side of the road waiting and hoping someone would stop to offer to help. Sometimes the wait seemed like forever. Occasionally, someone would stop right away and offer to help or make a phone call when he got home. Relieved, you would find a scrap piece of paper, scribble the name of someone and his number (you actually knew his number!), and express much thanks. If you were stuck and no one stopped, you would have to dig through the car for some change and start walking toward a pay phone. (Yes! They had phones you could insert coins in to make a call back then!) Hopefully, the walk was not too far. Finally, the really brave or really crazy person would put up his thumb and try to hitch a ride to the nearest place to call for help. You needed other people to get help. You were grateful for anyone who offered or came to your rescue. Cell phones changed all of this.

Today, it is a completely different story when people are

stranded. In my mind's eye, I can see three different groups of people and their responses when coming upon a broken down car or stranded driver. The first group of people are those who pass by without giving it a second thought. These are the same people who would have passed by back in my day. They always pass by, probably for many different reasons.

The second group of people will also pass by the stalled vehicle. This group assumes the driver or someone in the group has a cell phone. They say to themselves, "Everyone has a cell phone these days; there is no need to stop." They count it lucky for the driver to be living at a time when all have the ability to secure help on their own. This group also feels relieved they do not need to feel any guilt about not stopping. They are grateful they don't have to worry about others stuck on the side of the road.

The third group of people are similar to the second. They also assume someone in the party has a cell phone. However, this group of people will feel a pull inside to help. So they will slow down, look carefully, and try to confirm someone in the group is holding or using a cell phone. With confirmation, these drivers speed away, reassured that everything will be okay and help must be on the way. This third group of people is made up of people who would stop if really needed, but they want to know their help is really needed.

There may be other groups, but I would like to suggest we really need a fourth group. We need a group to stop regardless of whether there is a cell phone in the party—no assumptions, no excuses, and no checking and then speeding away. We need people who just stop and check with the stranded group and offer to help. In my opinion, we all need to want to be in this group.

We live in a fast-paced world, quickly becoming a global society. We would think because of technology we would become a more close-knit large village of humans anxious to help and bless each other. Yet, as in the case of stranded cars today, we tend to speed by, having a multitude of reasons not to stop and offer help. Of course, there are many great initiatives and actions to help others in this world, but all too often, people no longer make the spur of the moment decision to help someone else in need. We could be in any of the above three groups, but regardless, we still drive on by.

What would happen if we all strived to be someone who would stop no matter what? What if we worked to develop the kind of character where we felt the pull to offer assistance, even if outward evidence indicated it might not really be needed? Anyone who has ever been stranded and helped by a caring passerby has felt the surge of gratitude and renewed faith in other people. Let's face it! It feels good to be helped by another person when we are really in need.

Yet there is an even greater feeling than being helped. It is the feeling that comes when we deliver the help. Many of us have felt this feeling. There is nothing greater than knowing, because of you, someone else was saved from some kind of hardship or difficulty. It feels grand inside to give freely to others. When we give unselfish service to others, we seem to change inside. Our nature seems to soften, and our heart seems to grow. It is not just a warm feeling; our very capacity for charity increases. We literally become better people.

We don't just claim the blessing of being a giver. Because we helped someone else, we have more to give. When we give, we never lose anything; we gain everything. We find we are more than we thought we were. It is strengthening.

Might I suggest we all seek to be in the fourth group? Let's all try an experiment and stop any time we see someone in need. Let's make a resolution to notice and stop and help those we see on the side of the roads of life. Let's not make an excuse when we see people probably don't really need our help. Let's determine to stop because we need the experience of offering the help. Then, if desired and needed, let's give the help. Then we can watch and see what happens. I am persuaded we will all become better people. I am convinced the world will become a brighter place. Even if we don't really have as many opportunities to offer unselfish help and concern, we will be blessed for every effort we make to reach out and offer. We will become better because we were willing. We will find more of ourselves and this will bring greater happiness in life.

Next time you see someone stranded somewhere on the road of life, don't worry about whether he or she needs your help. Tell yourself *you* need to offer the help.

Chapter 24

Giving Your Old Car Away

I am one of those old people who listens to talk radio. When I was younger, I figured old people were the way they were because they listened to boring talk radio. Now I am one of those people. Frequently, as I am enjoying my talk radio, I hear promotions from non-profit organizations and even the station itself asking me to donate my car. To me, this seems like the latest thing—give your car away to support a good cause! They say it will be easy, it will really make a difference, and it is a painless way to support their cause. I have actually given a car away, but not to a radio station. My car was never mentioned in a radio publicity segment saying, "Jim donated his car and helped support this radio station. If he can do it, you can too!" Actually, I never received any recognition for donating my car. That is precisely why it affected me so much.

I loved my old car. My wife and I purchased it and had accumulated over 250,000 miles on it. It was my commuting car. My mechanic said the engine was in great shape and would easily go farther. The rest of the car, especially the plastic part, was falling apart. I reached up one day to turn on the dome light and the plastic cover literally fell apart in my hands.

Some other plastic parts disintegrated in the same fashion. My car was not a luxury car, but I loved everything about it. It was *my* car; it was *a* car, and it did exactly what I needed it to do. It was reliable and saw me to work and back every day. I loved this car.

Then my work transferred me across the United States. We had to plan to get all of our belongings and our vehicles to the other side of the country. I wanted to take my car. My wife suggested it would not make the long drive. We looked into having it towed or hauled, but the cost was more than the car was worth. Ultimately, my wife prevailed and we decided not to take the car with us. I was sad, but I agreed to leave the car behind. But what to do with it?

At the time, we had a good friend whose son was struggling. He was trying to take care of his young wife and two children. He was struggling to make ends meet, and I believe his car was falling apart and not reliable. My wife and I discussed it and decided to give the car to him. We called him up and asked him whether we could give him our car. He and his wife were shocked and wanted to pay us for the car. We insisted on giving it to them. We signed the title, handed them the keys, and moved across the United States. I never heard how it worked out since we moved across the country. But it does not really matter because I will never forget how I felt knowing I was making someone else's life easier by giving away my car.

We should all give something big away! A powerful feeling happens when you take something you love and give it away. The feeling is even stronger when you do not get any credit for the act and it requires a little bit of struggle for you. Today, we live in a country where the majority of us are so very blessed. We can, if we choose, find so many things for which to be grateful. Most likely, we have more than we need. We may not be able to give away a car, but we all have something we can give away. Yet we don't have to have abundance to claim the benefits of giving something away.

Something changed inside me after I gave away my prized car. I began to be more excited to give away things. I found myself packing extra food just to give to the homeless man on the side of the road every day. I heard about some people who needed some blankets and clothes, so I took all the extra I had and gave them away. I learned of a good family who operated a makeshift donation center out of their home for people in need to claim items they desperately need. I took a bunch of my surplus stuff to them. I could not stop thinking about it. In fact, hardly a day goes by when I do not think about the car I gave away. Really! I think about the other stuff I gave away too!

What happened? I wish I could explain it, but something changed inside me when I gave my car to someone in need. The feeling was so incredible! The look on the young man's face, the confused smile as he wondered why we chose him and his family, and his kind of shocked gratitude as he accepted the title—I'll never forget any of this. It was not even that great of a car. It probably did not last much longer for him anyway. Yet the feeling of giving it to him changed something in me.

So now I want to give away things. Many times, it is not even about the person who may need what I have to give. When I gave away my car, I realized I needed to give things away not so much because other people needed my things. I came to see I should be giving things away because I need to give. It is not about the car anymore. It is about giving unselfishly to others. I was changed when I gave my car away. I think we all need more of this same experience.

What will you give away today?

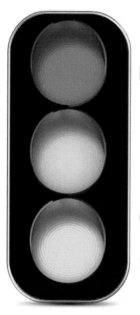

"THERE ARE VERY FEW PEOPLE WHO ARE SUCCESSFUL WHO DID NOT HAVE TO DO SOME SERIOUS DRAGGING TO GET THERE. ANY-THING WORTH-WHILE REQUIRES HARD WORK."

Chapter 25

Push, Pull, or Drag

I am not a big fan of car commercials. I mean, I like to see the new cars, but I do not like the ads. Most commonly, a local car dealer, whom it might be safe to guess has no prior acting experience, is pitching his dealership. He might be touting the great deals you will not find anywhere else. Another dealer shouts about having surplus cars that just have to be moved today. Each one brags about some great deal he just has to pass on to his customers. You can just feel the marketing pull. When has buying a car ever benefited any of us? Most people leave the dealership with increased debt and something that becomes a liability the minute you drive it off the lot. Sure, it is fun and we need a vehicle to get places, but are we really better off? One time, I really was!

I was just a couple of months away from my wedding day! I was so excited, planning one of the very best days of my life. My soon-to-be-bride was in town and we decided to go car shopping. She did not own a car and I owned an old, used car for which I had paid $600. This little car had been good for a time, but it had recently developed the nasty habit of breaking down in remote places and leaving me stranded. A couple of times, I was stuck and glad I had started carrying my bike in the back. It was winter, but at least I could get somewhere. Anyway, the old car had to go.

My sweetheart and I found the car we wanted and arranged to purchase it. The eager salesperson wondered whether we had a trade. We indicated we could bring in my little car. Of course, he inquired about the car's condition and I told him the truth. He acted as if it were no big deal and told us (the catchphrase we heard often from the car commercials): "Push, pull, or drag it in and we'll take it." That may have been the only true thing I ever heard in a commercial. So we arranged to bring my old car in. On that day, it started right up and we thought we were so blessed to get it to the dealership and get rid of it. However, as we pulled off the freeway to turn off toward the car lot, it died—right there with a huge line of cars behind us. Well, we pushed it and got it to the side of the road. Then, somehow we managed to get it rolling and limping its way to the dealership. We literally pushed, pulled, and dragged it into the lot. We were nervous about the whole "push-pull-drag" thing, but the guy smiled and welcomed us on the lot. He told us he was so glad we had managed to get the car there. I was a little surprised, completely relieved, and happy to hand him the keys. We unloaded the old car and drove away in our new one. It worked out.

Sometimes in life, we are carrying around habits and patterns that are not working out well for us. These habits or patterns often cause us to break down and not fully function to the best of our abilities. The habit or pattern may be an addiction to some sort of substance or practice. Occasionally, it is something like overeating and needing to lose weight. It may be not taking care of our body and failing to get proper exercise. It may be all of the above and more. At times, we all seem to find ourselves needing to change some bad habit that negatively affects us. We all have something we want and/or need to change.

The problem lies in the fact that change is hard. We all want to lose the "spare tire" we are carrying, but we also want to have just one more serving of our favorite dessert or treat. We all wish to be in better shape, but we also want to watch one more television show or movie. Surely, we all have some bad habit we need to change, but we also want to hang on to the things that make us comfortable and may even provide us escape from our other life challenges. We all feel the real need to change and become better, but we are not sure we are willing to make the effort to change. We may wonder whether we can even make the change. Maybe we tried in the past, but we failed to stick to our plan to change. Our resolutions became revolutions, and we were thrown back into our bad habits. Let's face it! It can be so very hard to make the changes we need to make.

At the risk of oversimplifying this situation, I believe the answer starts in the concept of "Push, pull, or drag." Often, these steps are the beginning, middle, and end of changing our lives and the habits that irritate and even plague us. Yet with just the right mix of push, pull, and drag, we can and will make changes. Let's talk for a moment about how this might help.

Push. First, we need to stop and look at what things in our life may be pushing us toward the addictive behavior or undesired habit. Usually, the actual addictive behavior is at the end of the line. The addictive behavior is not the *real* problem. It is the last part in a chain of behaviors, difficulties, or challenges. It is like when you were a little child and sitting at the top of the slide. You were afraid to go down, but it was a little too late. With a little push from the kid behind you, you were going down. It did not matter whether the slide was too hot, covered in dirt and mud, or leading to a puddle at the bottom. You were going down. The best help came from discovering what pushed you up the ladder to begin with.

It is actually quite simple. Push factors are going to be in one of four categories: emotions, thoughts, behaviors, or circumstances. All addictive behaviors or automatic habits are going to be preceded by one or more of these things. So you might ask yourself questions like: "What was I feeling before this happened? What thoughts did I have that made it easier to get stuck in my old habits? What behaviors did I engage in that often preceded my bad habit? What circumstances happened today to push me closer to this action or habit?" By stopping to look at what is really pushing us to these actions and habits, we can begin to see patterns and trends in our behaviors. When we see the push patterns, we begin to see where we can make changes. Then, we may be less likely just to feel like we have to come up with a way to quit. We will see the reasons and causes, or "push" to go to those things we so desperately want to stop or change. We can then get to work to change those things. Family, friends, church leaders, support groups, and counselors can really help at this point.

Pull. Second, we need to look at pull factors. This is the process of identifying the things that motivate us to make the change in our life. Pull factors are the reasons for making the change. These are the answer to "Why should I change?" The stronger the pull to change, the more likelihood of success. So, for instance, my main motivation for exercising is being healthy enough to play with my kids, my future grandkids, and to serve and help others. You see, I don't really like exercise. I like the results, but I dislike how I feel during and after exercise. Yet the pull to be healthy for my family and for the pleasure of serving others really motivates me. I think of it all the time. Pull factors are those things that will motivate you. So stop and ask yourself the real reasons you want to make this change (and in some cases, *need* to make the change). Make a list of those things. I had a coworker once who would create a collage of those reasons and hang it in a very visible place. When you know and feel strongly about the *why* behind the change you are making, it will help pull you to success.

Drag. The final part of our formula is drag. I am going to be blunt and honest here. A certain amount of any meaningful change involves hard work. So to be direct, drag means you have to drag yourself out of bed, off the couch, out of the comfortable seat, away from the fridge, away from the store, or wherever. I know very few people who are successful who did not have to do some serious dragging to get there. Let's be straight here! Anything worthwhile requires hard work. I repeat, anything worthwhile requires hard work. The best things in life are not free. As I look back on my life, the things I truly treasure most are those I earned by hard work, sweat, and persistent effort. I am and will be forever grateful that I learned to work hard. I also learned to keep going when things got tough. What valuable lessons! I learned to keep dragging myself back into the fight every day. I learned to keep dragging myself away from that which I ought not to do so I could do more of what I wanted to do or needed to do. Drag is counting the cost, making the sacrifice, and pushing all you can forward. Combined with an understanding of push and pull factors, drag becomes easier as you get to work. No amount of insight, knowledge, hope, faith, or even desperation is going to make the change for you, if not combined with dragging yourself to the battle and fighting on.

So if you are carrying around behaviors, habits, or patterns you would like to get rid of, it may be time to push, pull, and drag. Do these until you are finally ready to drop them off and replace them with something new and better. It will happen. It will be exciting as you "drive off" better, stronger, smarter, and more confident.

"WHEN YOU SAW WHAT YOU WANTED TO SEE, YOU PROBABLY MISSED WHAT YOU NEEDED TO SEE."

Chapter 26

Wondering Whether Everyone Drives One of These

It has always amazed me how buying a new car affects people. Some people are so ecstatic and want to tell everyone. Others are kind of quiet about it and only say something if asked, "Hey! Did you get a new car?" For some people, it is a big deal while for others it really doesn't matter much. To me, one of the most interesting parts of having a new car comes about two weeks after I purchase the car and I am starting to get used to it. This phenomenon surprised me the first couple of times our family obtained a new car. Now, I am prepared for it.

What is the phenomenon? It happens when I am driving my two-week old car and I suddenly begin to see all the other cars on the road that look exactly like my new car. When I drove a black minivan, I saw a ton of black minivans just like it. When I drove the little blue sedan, it seemed like everywhere I went, someone had a perfect match for my little blue sedan. Red four-door? Presto! Everyone drives one of these. No matter what the type of car has been, I will have the guaranteed experience of finding all the other cars just like mine on the road. I used to figure it was because cool people like what I like. However, when my car was older and broken down, I saw other cars similar to it. So it was not just me being in some elite group of cool-same-choice-in-car people. Something else was going on. I was seeing what I wanted to see. Having my car opened me up to seeing those cars like mine. It is something I will call "You see what you are looking for."

Life is really interesting in this regard. We all tend to see the things we want to see. Just this morning, I experienced an example of this phenomenon. I went in to awaken my daughter for the day. Not liking this time of day, she said to me, "I have been up all night. I had to get up to go to the bathroom and someone was in there taking a shower so I had to wait!" My daughter wanted to stay in bed. She asked whether she could please sleep a little longer because of having to be "up all night." She was citing the evidence to support her point of view. She felt she had a compelling argument for staying in bed. She was not happy when I did not share her point of view. Many of our own personal challenges may come from intentionally or unintentionally seeing what we want to see.

Let's take this example of my daughter a little further to illustrate the point. She has never seemed to like mornings. Every morning is hard for her to get up and get going. She has missed the bus many times because she was not ready. You could safely say that she is invested in staying in bed every day as long as she can. Thus, it is not unusual for her to make some request to stay in bed. Today, she had a new reason: someone was in the shower, so she could not use the bathroom, so she had to stay up. However, what her young brain missed because she was looking for a reason to stay in bed was my awareness of what time her older brother gets up. He had not been in the bathroom for very long. She maybe had missed a couple of minutes of sleep because of her bathroom excursion. She wanted it to be longer. She wanted to stay in bed. She saw it as a long time because of what she wanted.

How often do we do exactly as my daughter? We are in a particular mood, have certain preferences or desires, and are focused on getting the things we want. These desires influence us to see what we want to see on the roads of life. While not always problematic, this habit of seeing what we want to see can really create some difficulties for us. For instance, if we believe someone has treated us unfairly, we are more likely to see all the evidence that supports that conclusion. We see what we are looking for. When this happens, we are likely to do what I call "jumping to a confusion." If we proceed with seeing what we want to see, we may cause all kinds of bad stuff to happen and harbor all kinds of unpleasant feelings. In fact, many of life's relationship challenges come from this phenomenon. When we see what we want to see and react to it, we may just come to the wrong conclusion, miss some of the facts, and hurt ourselves or others. I have counseled hundreds of people who have jumped to confusions because they only saw what they wanted to see. A world of hurt can come if we are not careful in this regard.

So how do we keep from seeing what we want to see and having it create negative feelings and interpretations for us? I have learned that the solution lies in some introspection and honest questioning of myself. I will give a personal example. When I was in high school, I auditioned and made it into the top jazz band. I became the section leader and loved playing in this group. Because I was section lead, I really wanted to have the opportunity to play a feature solo. I had observed other lead players getting this opportunity, and it was most certainly not uncommon in this type of band. So I asked the director about it. He offered me a kind word and said, "You will get your chance!" He then explained that I had more years of school to go, so he was going to let the upperclassmen have this chance, but he assured me that when I was an upperclassman, he would select me. Well, the last semester of my senior year, it had not happened yet. I was almost out of time. So I asked again. He brushed me off, told me he was going to feature the piano player, and did not remember his promise to me a couple of years earlier. I would not be playing a feature number.

I was very angry and very hurt. I felt betrayed, and I immediately felt a loss of respect for my director. I believed he had lied to me, and I never wanted to trust him again. Our relationship became cold and distant, and I began to avoid him. Also, I gave up working as hard on my music. I began to lose interest and be annoyed at even having to be in music class, let alone be near the man who had hurt me so much. I was angry, and it was his fault. I began to see all the unfair things he did, and I was just incensed about it all. He was ruining my goals for my music and my life. He had promised, but now he was being so unfair and wrong.

You might be tempted to side with me and agree that I was wronged, so I had reason to be upset. You may be able to see my point of view. It was years later before I chose to take another look at this whole event. This time, I decided to tell the story from another point of view. I started by asking myself, "In telling this story (over and over again), have I in any way omitted any important details?" After reflecting on it, I also asked myself "Am I being a victim in any way in telling this story?" I really wanted to look at it in another way so I could stop being upset about it. This decision is what made the difference. I was, in fact, leaving out some key parts of the story. The details are not important, but when I chose to see what I was most definitely not seeing, I had a different experience. I began to see the pressures on an underpaid high school band teacher. I began to see the incredible talents of my best friend who had only been in the band for a year and had never had as many opportunities as I had (having been in the band my entire high school career) and how this opportunity helped her and built her confidence. Even more, I began to see how much I had gained by not getting what I wanted. Perhaps, there were some lessons I needed to learn. I have only listed a couple of examples, but I learned so much more. It was an incredible growth experience to make myself see something not as easy to see. When I saw it, it changed me. I needed this change in my life. It was worth the effort to see what I had not been seeing.

Life moves quickly. We often have to make quick judgments and decisions about things. We also have a lot we can react to as life events come at us every day. Let's face it! At the pace of today's life, it is really much easier to see what you want to see and just keep moving. It is easier just to view people through our own limited lenses rather than slowing down and trying to see more of the story. Let's be honest; it does not take much effort to conclude that someone treated us unfairly, wronged us, or that something is unfair. Snap judgments are exactly that! We can make them quickly and easily. Then, we think we are justified in how we respond and react to what comes next. We can too easily convince ourselves that our course is right and we should feel the way we do.

It takes much more effort and maturity to slow down and see another interpretation, examine another point of view, and search from a different vantage point. In fact, it takes incredible courage to be willing to look at something to see whether there is another way of seeing things. The willingness to step into another place and get a different angle can produce powerful results. This energy directed toward a broader understanding of all that happened or happens can produce a whole array of new feelings. If you are seeking peace and rest over events in life that trouble you, anger you, or eat at you, then you may benefit from taking another look. Instead of seeing that usual, familiar thing, try to see something else. Allow yourself to explore it from any other vantage point. Try hard to see a different part of the story. You may just be surprised what happens when the new scene unfolds. It may just not be what you thought it was. When you saw what you wanted to see, you probably missed what you needed to see.

"WE ALL NEED TO LEARN TO LOVE AND VALUE CORRECTIVE FEEDBACK FROM THOSE WE TRUST."

Chapter 27

Watching Out for the Mechanic
Under Your Hood

Whenever my car breaks down, I always do the same thing. I pop the hood, get out of the car, struggle to find the hidden latch, and look to see what is wrong. This is laughable because I don't know a thing about cars. I *do* know how to add fuel and washer fluid and to check the oil, but none of those skills has ever helped me when stranded. Otherwise, I guess I am hoping a little flag will shoot out pointing to the source of the difficulty. It would be nice if it were accompanied by instructions to push a green reset button. That has never happened, but it would sure be nice. Truth be told, I don't know why I pop the hood. Even if I somehow found the source of the problem, I lack the skills to repair my car. I imagine, like most people, I am dependent on a mechanic to maintain my car. A good mechanic is required by almost all of us. Those who know how to repair their own cars are truly blessed indeed!

I have had many experiences with mechanics. I am appreciative of their skills and knowledge about my car's workings. It impresses me how they can know what is going on and then determine solutions. Yet I have struggled with the actions of some of the mechanics who have worked on my car and fixed things I didn't want to be fixed. Recently, I arranged an online appointment with the people who normally fix my car. The online worksheet asked what I wanted done. I checked the appropriate boxes and typed in some additional comments on what I was requesting. I received the confirmation of the appointment, which repeated my service request. When I dropped off the car, the attendant confirmed my request and took my keys. I even signed a form giving my permission for the mechanics to work on the things I asked them to work on. Everything was moving along smoothly. Or so I thought.

A short time later, I received a phone call. The mechanic on the other end listed off the things needing attention on my car, none of which were things on my request list. He told me how much it would cost to repair these items and asked whether they could go ahead with the work. Puzzled, I thanked him for his work and inquired about the status of the things I wanted done. He responded with equal confusion and noted he did not look at those things. I responded, "I would like those things done, thank you." He assured me he would look into those things "right away" and get back to me. A short time later, he called back mentioning a few of the items on my list, but not all of them. I asked again whether he could look at ALL of my list. He apologized and said again he would report back. In the meantime, without my authorization, the mechanic did the work on *his* original list. Finally, after what seemed like forever, I received a call with the news that my car was ready. I arranged a ride and went to pick it up.

Imagine my surprise when I discovered that *none* of the things

I wanted had been done! Of course, I was not happy to receive a bill for all these things I did not want done. Then, I still needed the other stuff to be done. So I asked for the manager. He pulled up the original request, the confirmation, and the signed confirmation. He tried to make it right. I had to leave my car for a couple of more hours to get done what I originally wanted done. It was frustrating. I wish this had not happened. I wish it did not happen often.

You see, I recognize I am not educated about what my car needs. I don't feel any feelings of inferiority or inadequacy about this. I don't mind getting help, and I am not afraid of asking for what I need. I will get recommendations I feel good with, and I will follow through with those I wish and prioritize how I want to address them. I love knowing I can call on someone with expertise to help me. I consider it intelligence to seek help when you need it. I don't mind asking for help.

Yet I think I am like most people when it comes to asking for help. Once we get to the point of asking, we don't want help we weren't asking for. If I take an honest look at myself and my life, I could probably improve upon over a hundred things. Ask my wife and kids and they will likely tell you a hundred is a gross underestimate. I have work I can do. I have imperfections and flaws pretty much everywhere. I am not naive about this. I am a very goal-oriented and driven person. I love to work on getting better. Again, I am also not afraid of asking for the help and input of others when I need help. I find asking for feedback and advice a great experience. I like to ask for feedback, and I look forward to getting it. I have learned growth from feedback works so much better when I seek it.

But here is my point: When I ask for feedback, I don't want someone to dump the whole load of hay on me. I really don't like having someone lift my hood and say, "Well, while we're in here, you should also probably work on this!" It just does not go over as well. I appreciate someone being able to see and know my weaknesses. I appreciate people who might be better at something I struggle with. Even more, I love those among my trusted friends and family who have given me counsel, correction, and helpful advice in my times of need. I just notice my most trusted friends and those who have helped me the most are the ones who only give me just what I was asking for. They help me where I am ready to be helped. They give me what I can afford at that time. Consequently, when I am ready, I will return to them for more. When they helped me with what I needed, I came to trust them. When I returned and it went well again, I became a loyal customer. My best friends are those who help me with what I need help with. I appreciate this so much. My life has been bettered because of this kind of love and kindness from others. I have learned to love and value corrective feedback from those I trust. Many of my good points have come about because of loving feedback and help from others.

So when you look under my hood, I already know you will find something I can get to work on. Will you please help me to work on what I want to work on? I will do all I can afford to do at that time. When I have more and am more, then let's talk more about what you see. I will be able to take care of it then.

"WHAT IF INSTEAD OF NOTICING AND FOCUSING ENTIRELY ON WHEN THINGS GO WRONG, WE FOCUSED ON WAYS TO FIND OUT WHETHER WE ARE DOING WELL?"

Chapter 28

Idiot Lights

I am not sure whether the title of this chapter is unique to my family or whether others have used this phrase as well. I don't recall ever hearing it from others. My family has used this phrase for as long as I can remember. "Idiot lights" is what we have come to call the lights on our car's dashboard. Most of the time, no lights are shining or blinking on the dashboard. However, when something is wrong, the lights come on. You may find an oil light, an engine light, and more. As technology advances, so do our cars' indicator or "idiot" lights. I feel like an idiot when I can't determine what the picture is supposed to represent. I have to find the manual and look it up.

Once, I was driving a company car when this odd looking light came on. I could not figure out what it was. It looked like someone pressing down on three pieces of bacon. (I like bacon, but I did not know what it had to do with the vehicle!) I finally found the picture in the manual and learned the tire pressure was dangerously low on one of my tires. I did not know which one, but it was low. The manual said to get it filled immediately. So, a little concerned, I searched for a place to fill the tires. I was a little worried I might be ruining my tires by continuing to drive, but I had to get somewhere

I could get air. I finally found a place where the staff checked the tires and filled them up. I was assured my car was good to go now. Yet just a short drive away from the place, the light came back on. Again, feeling like an idiot, I rechecked the manual and it still said the bacon slices meant the tires were dangerously low. I did not know what to do. After about a month of looking at bacon slices, I took the car to the dealership. The guy there said, "Oh, your spare tire probably needs air in it too!" Sure enough, he filled it up and the light went off. Who knew? I never thought of that and felt kind of like an idiot. At least now, when the bacon light comes on, I know to check all five of the tires on that car!

My family calls these lights "idiot lights" because they are not really helpful (aside from the fact that they look like bacon!). A light coming on to tell you something really bad has just occurred is not really helpful. For example, one of my little cars has an oil light that only comes on when the car is completely out of oil. As you already know, I don't know much about cars. However, I do know that if my car is completely out of oil, I am already destroying my engine before the light even comes on! To me, that is idiotic, not helpful. I am glad to know I have already begun to destroy my engine—would have been nice to know sooner. I am glad to know I am already destroying my tires by continuing to drive on them—would have been nice to know I had a flat before I got to this point.

Now I know some of you are saying or thinking, "Well, if you would just check your oil every time you fill up your car with gas, you would never have to worry." I get that. You are right. Yet for whatever reason, I was born at a time when we have all kinds of wonderful technology to help us live better lives. Since we have it, I would like to use it. I would love it if it were really and truly helpful. An indicator light flashing when my oil level is a quart low or when the tires are just a little low in pressure would be excellent. Some cars have gauges that are always telling you how much oil or power you have left. Yet even some of these gauges are written in some strange language I cannot understand. If these idiot lights were really meant to be helpful, they would tell us exactly what we needed to know. A light that says, "Add 1 quart oil soon" would be helpful. A gauge that tells me I have two weeks of battery power left would be very nice.

I have been blessed in my life with some friends and family members who are like gauges for me. One day, my wife and kids noticed a powerful gauge that has blessed my life tremendously. They noticed the only time I am ever grumpy is when I am too tired. I appreciate this discovery. I tended to find fault with myself when I could not get everything done so I pushed myself harder and harder. Then, when I found myself getting irritated and short with loved ones, I felt guilty about it all. I did not really see what was going on. When they pointed it out to me, it was so very helpful. Now, they work with me to see this. We have laughed together when I am being a little crabby and one of my family will say, "Should we send Daddy to bed early tonight?" Instead of lecturing me, fighting with me, telling me I am a jerk, or worse, they remind me I am human and need to get rest. I like this response because I find I am not offended, I don't turn toward being self-critical, and I hear a helpful message. If they told me to stop being an idiot, I would probably not feel good inside, be defensive, and talk negatively to myself. When they lovingly gauge what I am doing, I see what needs to change and I can make that change. It is very helpful for me. It saves me from feeling and acting like an idiot. I like that!

We have too many things and too many people in our lives telling us we messed up. Often those messages come from inside ourselves. We are quick to find fault in others and even more often in ourselves. What if instead of noticing and focusing entirely on when things go wrong, we focused on ways to find out whether we are doing well? What if instead of idiot lights in our thoughts and self-talk, we installed some gauges? What if we focused on figuring out what is going well and then zeroed in on things that would let us know whether things were starting to go south? We need more helpful gauges in our lives. We need more personal and interpersonal measures to help us support each other before things get to burn up or burn out.

Now if I could just get me some bacon to go with it!

"THE WORLD HAS PLENTY OF PEOPLE WHO USE THEIR HANDS TO HURT. WE NEED MORE PEOPLE WHO USE THEM TO HELP. THERE ARE ENOUGH PEOPLE IN THIS WORLD WHO USE THEIR HANDS TO BREAK DOWN. WE NEED MORE PEOPLE TO USE THEIR HANDS TO LIFT UP. THERE ARE TOO MANY WHOSE HANDS ARE HARD. WE NEED HANDS THAT ARE SOFT. WE NEED HANDS READY TO LIFT, TO BUILD, TO STRENGTHEN, TO SERVE, AND TO SUPPORT. WE NEED HANDS TO HOLD."

Chapter 29

Watching for Yellow Lights

Traffic lights are just not what they used to be. When I was a kid, we were taught in detail the purposes of each of the different colors on the traffic signal. Red most definitely meant stop. It was a clear message for cars to stop any forward movement. Yellow lights were yield. They meant to slow down and prepare to stop. In short, yellow's job was to say, "Take it easy! Here comes Red!" Green meant it was safe to go forward. Green is everyone's favorite.

Today, these colors seem to mean something entirely different than the traffic lights of my childhood. Red seems to mean "Hurry and get as many cars through before the people going the other direction start out." Instead of the clear "Stop!" message of my childhood, red seems to be viewed by folks as more of an advisory or option. Most people seem to get the message, "Hey! It might be a good idea to stop now if it is convenient for you." Tons of money is spent annually to try to challenge this notion with so-called red light cameras. Red just don't get no R-E-S-P-E-C-T anymore. Yellow has definitely stopped being a yield or slow down message. Far from meaning to be cautious and careful, yellow now says to people, "Step on it, man! Here comes Red!" Yellow seems to invoke anything but what it was intended to say. Green has also changed. It is not just the "Go" message it used to be. It also seems to carry a caution message because someone might be selectively color-blind to red and thus be zooming through your safe green zone. The green zone is no longer a zone of safety. It may mean it is safe to go forward, but it might not. So green is now more "Take your chances! It might be safe! It is the best guess of the universe whether we are safe this time at this intersection." Green does not boast as much confidence as she used to have. Green is a gamble now.

I would love to see all of the traffic lights get back to their original strength and power. Whenever I see an accident, obviously caused by not following the traffic signal, I feel sad inside. I wish all traffic lights were taken as seriously as they were when I was a child. However, for this chapter, I just want to advocate getting yellow back to its original strength and purposes. To me, yellow is the best light in the world. I believe we need more yellow lights in our lives. I also believe we need to see them more clearly.

As we travel through life, it is so very helpful to know "red lights" in our life. These are the signals telling us we are doing things we should not or do not want to be doing. Red lights can indicate forbidden areas where we have decided to stop. For some, red lights are things like alcohol or drugs, unsafe practices, and other actions or activities the person has decided he does not want in his life. A good red light list tells you to stop and not go in those directions. A good green light list tells you the good things you want to and can be doing each day. Green says these things are good, healthy, productive, and help you feel better. We can have green diets, green exercise programs, and green hobbies. When life is in the green zone, we are happier. When we slide into red, we are unhappy and unhealthy. This is why yellow is so important.

A good list of your personal or family's yellow lights can really help to avoid hard times and difficulties. When you know what your personal and family yellow lights are, you can slow down and make changes. I will give a couple of personal examples to illustrate how recognizing a yellow light can help you to be a better and healthier person. When family or friends are involved, they help too! These yellow lights may seem silly to you, but they work. They warn me that if I do not stop soon, I will surely end up in my red zone.

The first yellow light I have found is what happens first thing in the morning. I am either blessed or cursed with the ability to wake up without an alarm clock in the morning. Usually, I wake up very early and at least five minutes before my alarm goes off, no matter what time I set it to go off. This is green for me. Very occasionally, what normally happens for me does not happen. I sleep either all the way to my alarm or I hit the snooze button and stay in bed. This is my yellow light. I have talked to my wife about it. Whenever she or I notice this yellow light, we know I am either too stressed, too tired, or something is wrong. I need to slow down and take care of something. For me, it is almost always needing more rest. It could be an indicator I am coming down with some kind of illness. My wife might say something to me like, "Hey, hon! You asked me to tell you when I saw a yellow light. Just wanted you to know I saw one this morning. I love you." She does not even have to tell me what she saw. She just points out (like she might when we are driving), "Hey!

The light was yellow back there!" This information is helpful because she cannot fix whatever it is, but she is supporting me and working with me. Also, I bear full responsibility for seeing the yellow light and paying attention to it. I am the driver. It is up to me to slow down and fix it. If I do, I almost always keep the red from happening.

The second example is kind of personal and funny! I am almost afraid to share it because it might change your opinion of me. Yet it is a powerful, personal yellow light for me. It is my face breaking out. I thought I was done with acne when I left my teenage years in the dust, but I was wrong. My face still breaks out. Yet one day, I noticed a helpful pattern. My face only breaks out into teenage trauma when I am about to get sick. My face will break out, and then I will get sick. It happens virtually every time. So, my face breaking out became the yellow light for the red light of getting sick. Can you guess what this information has done for me? I have learned how to prevent many of the sick days I have in my life. If I notice my face breaking out, I can immediately make health corrections and often prevent the red. I find it cool such a small yellow light helps me to prevent many of the illnesses I used to have. In the past, I felt powerless and stuck. Now, I see a way I can slow down and prevent. It works well!

Yellow lights can be just about anything. If I am not currently reading a book, I am probably too stressed. Yellow light. If I am channel surfing, I am probably overwhelmed with something. Yellow light. If I am taking too many naps, I have probably taken too much upon myself. Yellow light. If I pay close attention to these yellow lights, I am warned in advance, so I can slow down and make positive changes to avoid a red moment or experience. It is so helpful.

So would you take some advice from me? Sit down and make up your red light list. Jot down all the things you wish you did not do and the things that indicate you are unhappy or unhealthy. Then, skip to green and write down all the things you normally do when you are feeling the happiest and healthiest. The yellow list will be the hardest to make. It may take you some time to pay attention to what happens between your green and red lists. You may have to look carefully for anything that could indicate the switch is happening. It may be helpful to ask a trusted friend questions like "What do you observe happening to me right before I start doing my red things?" Listen carefully and see whether something comes to light. Make the yellow light list and learn to pay heed to it. You will find yourself better able to stop the red lights from happening. This is powerful!

Once you have determined your yellow lights for yourself, consider doing this activity as a couple or as a family. You could sit down together and brainstorm all the good, green light things you do together when you are happiest and healthiest. Then, list the red lights that tell you things are most assuredly not well. Then, challenge everyone to look for the yellow lights. You might ask, "What kinds of things seem to happen before we get to these red light items?" Then list them and work together to point them out. Your children will say things like "I see a yellow light! I see a yellow light!" Then, everyone can smile, regroup, and change.

There is power in following and honoring the true intention and purpose behind all of the colors on the traffic signal. I believe yellow is the most powerful. When you know the yellow light, you can better handle life and get quickly back to green. It just works well to be paying attention for yellow lights. So if you ever see me around, ask me what I am reading. If I cannot tell you, let me know you see a yellow light. If my face happens to be breaking out, please don't make fun of me. Let me know in a kind way that you see a yellow light. I will appreciate the reminder and it will help me to slow down and get back to green.

"OUT OF ALL GOD'S CREATURES, WE ARE THE ONLY ONES WHO HAVE THE FULL CAPACITY TO CHOOSE, IN ANY SET OF CIRCUMSTANCES, HOW WE WILL ACT, HOW WE WILL RESPOND."

Chapter 30

Getting into Tailgating

Have you ever been in a huge hurry to get somewhere but end up behind the slowest car in the world? Why are slow people always driving when you need to get somewhere? You wish you could get around them, but they are always in front of you when there is no possible way to pass. If you are a driver, you have been there and done this! You hate it! We all do! You are tailgating, but not the fun way. You are most certainly not with a group of friends going to some fun event. You are stuck, and the only thing you can think of to do is ride close to the person in front of you, hoping he or she will somehow get the message to speed up, pull over, or get sucked into a large portal opened specifically by the universe to swallow drivers who make you late! This is when you wish your car had one of those cool buttons where you could launch powerful rockets into the car in front of you so you wouldn't be hindered anymore.

We all tailgate at times. I can think of three primary times where tailgating happens, two of them planned, acceptable, and not too stressful, and one of them, unplanned, stressful, and enough to make you hate getting behind the wheel of the car. I am betting you did not realize there were times you got in a tailgate situation and you were not stressed out. This says something about tailgating—more than we might think in the moment because, generally, we don't like to be stuck behind someone. Or at least it would seem so.

A tailgate party is an experience where you follow a group of people to a fun event. Almost always, this is a planned event. My family used to love to do these when I was a kid. I am from the Mile High City, so it was a big deal to take a tailgate party to the Denver Broncos games. It still is. I can remember people and cars, decked out in orange and blue, heading excitedly down the road. Cars were honking, and orange faces stuck out of windows and gave a holler! This was pure fun! Often the cars would end up all together in the parking lot, and the coolers, the barbeque grills, and the great food came out. It was always a good time!

A funeral is another time when we follow other drivers closely. I can still remember the first time I went to a funeral as a child. It was for my great-aunt Eva. To be honest, I don't remember even meeting her. After I saw her in the coffin (my first time seeing a dead person), I hoped I did not know her. It was kind of creepy. I felt sad she had died. I did not have any memories of her, but everyone else was sad. It was my first experience with grief and loss. What came next was the caravan to the graveside service. The cars all lined up behind the hearse and the family limousines. Back then, the city would provide a complimentary escort by at least three motorcycle cops. It was cool to watch them. I was not at all frustrated with the experience of the slow, bumper-to-bumper ride to the graveside. I was fascinated watching the whole event. The procession was led by one of the policemen. He would turn on his lights and push on, blasting the siren at intersections. Then, at the intersection, he would park in the middle and stop all the traffic. Then, the coolest thing, one of his partners would come flying up the side of the procession and take the lead. They alternated this procedure until we were all safely at the cemetery. I loved the revving up of the motorcycle engine as police motorcycles shot up the line to be in front. My young heart raced with the excitement of it all. I tried not to get too excited because this was a funeral, but either way you look at it, this was cool! I was not anxious to go to more funerals, but I will never forget my childhood experience going to funerals and riding in the caravan with police escort. That experience of "tailgating" has never bothered me. To be honest, I still get a little excited inside when I see the escorts (now optional, hired, and minus the cool sirens).

The stress-inducing, blood-pressure-raising type of tailgating is when you are stuck behind someone moving slower than you wish to go. For some, this situation produces incredible dashboard-pounding, curse-word-using, stress. I have observed people yelling, leveling unkind words to drivers, and literally pulling at their hair. Not a desired experience, yet the experience is the same as the two mentioned above. We are behind a line of cars. But something is going on inside us that makes this latter event painful and even agonizing for us. What is that difference? What can we do about it?

The key difference is inside us. Would you believe you can be stuck behind a slow-moving person and be as cheerful as you are in a tailgate party? As calm as you are in a funeral procession? How is such a thing possible? I sometimes call it intelligent, voluntary choice. Out of all God's creatures, we are the only ones who have the full capacity to choose, in any set of circumstances, how we will act, how we will respond. There is incredible power in harnessing the freedom to choose.

Many times in life, we just follow, taking no thought for what we are doing and why we are doing it. There can be great danger in blindly following. Many are the stories of individuals who have been harmed by mindlessly following someone, not thinking of where things might be leading. It takes effort and energy to master the power of intelligent, voluntary choice. We start by recognizing this incredible capacity within us. Then, we harness that power. Believe it or not, we can be as calm as a summer morning in whatever circumstance we are in. Next, we talk to ourselves. We communicate positive messages, honest messages to ourselves about the situation we are in. The main difference between the tailgate party or funeral procession and being stuck behind someone is what we tell ourselves. Pay attention next time. You can tell yourself different messages. I find, for me, most of the time when I am stressed behind someone, I am artificially inflating the urgency. Most of the time I am not late and I did not really need to be worried. When I have occasionally been late, it has rarely ever been a big deal. So most of my stress was self-imposed. A calm, soothing message like "It will be okay" or "Getting angry about it is not going to make the car move any faster" can really help. Realistic, positive self-talk can help to harness this intelligent voluntary choice. We begin to tap into the incredible power of our mind to make things right, better, calm, etc. Some people have learned to have fun with it. Your mind is so powerful you could even imagine the stuck-in-traffic-time turning into a tailgate party. You could calm yourself by thinking the way you would in a ride to the cemetery. You are the master of your thoughts. Instead of just following along in frustration, is it time to take control?

Don't just be a follower, and don't lose your self-control when you find yourself momentarily stuck following someone. Make the intelligent voluntary choice to take charge of yourself and your mind. You can do this!

Chapter 31

Knowing There Is Something Better Than "The Bird"

I have tried to imagine this: Two people, a very long time ago, are racing their chariots to the local market. All of a sudden, a small peasant wagon pulls in front of them and cuts the leader off. He is forced to drive his cart on to the side of the road. His opponent continues on, waving victoriously. What does the unfortunate loser do? He gets angry and turns to the person who cut him off. He cannot think of anything else to do. So he curses something and points his middle finger in the air. Thus, "flipping the bird" was invented. I cannot even imagine how the name originated. Maybe the peasant was simple-minded and actually thought the angry driver was holding a bird. Who knows? Perhaps archeologists found people frozen in some odd state with their middle finger up. Then trying to explain this phenomenon, they came up with some complex explanation. Well, it stuck. Unfortunately, so has this gesture.

I am going to ask a favor. If you have the habit of making this obscene gesture (or any of its cousin insulting gestures), please stop. Please stop now. This gesture is not doing anything for you. Rude finger gestures, like profanity, only show a person is not in control of himself and not using his full intelligence to handle a situation. It does not make other people look bad when you do this. It makes you look bad. Imagine for a moment getting upset at a driver who cuts you off. You begin to raise your hand into this gesture, but just before you make it, you recognize the other driver. What if it were your boss, a member of your church, or a good friend? How would you feel in that instance? This illustrates the true impact of an angered response such as this. Rude hand gestures are for people who cannot, have not, or will not take the time to come up with better things to do with their hands. Rude hand gestures say something about how much or how little you care about the feelings and thoughts of others. Flipping the bird has never produced good feelings or experiences. We don't like others when they respond in this manner. If we are honest, we don't really like ourselves when we get to this point. There are so many better things we can do.

Think about it! Our hands are quite remarkable. We have the ability to do an abundance of things because of four fingers and an opposable thumb. Our hands distinguish us from all other creatures. We are powerful because we have hands. Take a moment and look at your hands (unless you are driving!). Aren't they remarkable? Now, think for a moment of all the things your hands can do. The list probably seems endless. There is almost no limit to what human hands can do.

If you struggle with making these kinds of gestures, you can learn new ways to express yourself. For practice, you can do this at home with your family. Take turns coming up with new things to do with your hands. In our home, we often do these kinds of things at the dinner table. I can see a mock challenge. I imagine a parent challenging a child who struggles with making this rude gesture to a duel. I can see myself saying to one of my children, "Is that the best you can do?" Then, the challenge: "I bet I can come up with more things to do with my hands than you can!" Let the competition begin. Maybe I will shoot for a hundred things! We could go back and forth until we run out of ideas or laugh ourselves silly. In our family, while doing things like this, we have laughed until the milk comes out of our noses! We have so much fun. You could do it by category. First, you could do creative: Origami! Knitting! Shadow puppets! You could do gross: Pick your nose! Pick your friend's nose! How about animals? Jellyfish, turkey, albatross (admit you had to think about that one!). You get the picture! There is so much more that strong and intelligent hands can do.

Let's be real here! It is so easy just to mimic some rude gesture first concocted by someone centuries ago. It does not take much intellect to repeat these kinds of things. The world has plenty of people who use their hands to hurt. We need more people who use them to help. There are enough people in this world who use their hands to break down. We need more people to use their hands to lift up. There are too many whose hands are hard. We need hands that are soft. We need hands ready to lift, to build, to strengthen, to serve, and to support. We need hands to hold. Let's all show how smart we really are by doing something better with our hands. Let's practice doing good things with our hands—productive, happy, positive, intelligent things.

There, I already gave you a bunch of better-than-the-bird things your hands can do! What else can you come up with? Show me when you see me! Go!

Chapter 32

Resisting the Expectation to Break the Law for Others

As a boy, I was not very good at getting in trouble. I almost always had to have help. Fortunately, I was given an older brother who was kind enough to assist in this important endeavor. Chances are, if I were playing with my older brother, he would soon lead us to something we should not be doing. Most of the time, the ideas he came up with (and I have no idea how he came up with these things!) were more like pranks or jokes. Some of them were harmful and against the law, but I looked up to him and wanted to do whatever he did. This was not always very smart! I often just uttered, "Okay" when he would suggest these things. Then, I would blindly follow.

We lived on a large hill with a curvy road. There was a field behind our house. My brother suggested that we build a rock wall in the middle of the road just around the corner. He laughed as he described cars coming around the corner, down the hill, not having enough time to stop before hitting the wall. I said "Okay" and proceeded to carry the large rocks from the field. As I think about this, I am sure I was just slave labor. He was the genius behind all these less-than-wholesome activities. Unfortunately, I was too willing to follow. So I helped him build a rock wall in the middle of the road. At first, cars could swerve around a couple of rocks. Eventually, the wall started to get big. I should have seen it coming, but drivers started to be a little unhappy. They might have even given that bird gesture. I felt bad, but I kept going at my brother's insistence.

I am ashamed to say I followed my brother in doing a lot of things. He persuaded me to throw snowballs at the man driving the snowplow. This was my first experience being chased by someone who wanted to do me harm. I did not think I could actually hit the center of the driver's side of the windshield. What were the odds of that? I did not really have time to think about it. He turned and drove the plow our way. You can run fast in the snow when you have to do so.

I remember one Thanksgiving morning delivering newspapers. My brother had a paper route and the paper was delivered every Thursday morning. So that meant every Turkey Day, he was up early delivering papers. Again, I was his errand boy and occasional pack horse. Somehow he talked me into doing the route with him. So we trudged out in the ice cold to deliver papers. We were near the end of the route when we came upon the mean old man's house. My brother encouraged me to throw the paper from the street and hurry on. I was never good at throwing the paper, but this time I got a perfect spin. You know those old screen doors with the very large metal panels on the bottom? (Some of you could finish this story!) The panel was like the giant brass gong and the paper was the mallet making contact right in the center. Imagine that sound early in the morning on Thanksgiving.

Grumpy old man became very fast moving man. He came after us. We ran. He got into his truck. We split up. I left my brother behind. There was no way I was going to die on Thanksgiving before I had my share of turkey. To be truthful, I was terrified. I don't think I delivered papers with my brother anymore. He tried to talk me into collecting with him that month. There was no way I was going to go to the cymbal-house and face that man. I was done.

I am not proud to admit that I did other things with my brother, including stealing from local stores. At first, I was terrified, but he made it look so easy. Eventually, he persuaded me to take something. I was successful. We did it several more times. Then we were caught. The store owner called my mom. Unknown to us, she told him to scare us. He did it pretty well. I was banished from that store forever. I had an allowance and my mom not only made me pay for what I took (and give it back), but she also took me to every store I had stolen from and made me return the items and pay for them. I am grateful now for what my mom did. I had never liked how I felt inside. My short life of crime ended at that point. I was lucky in so many ways. First, it ended there. Second, I learned to tell the difference between someone encouraging me to do something wrong versus someone helping me do something right. This lesson has made all the difference for me.

So when you pull up behind me on the freeway and I am going the speed limit, please do not expect me to break the law for you. As soon as possible, I will pull over and let you pass me. I am not interested in keeping you from where you want to go, but I don't want to speed up and break the law. You see, I remember what it was like to get caught breaking the law. I also know what it feels like to have my conscience nag me. I don't like either experience. Also, I am pretty sure if a police officer comes up behind us and he stops me for speeding, you are not going to help me out. I am guessing you will slow down just long enough to laugh at me and speed away as soon as you believe it is clear. If I am caught, I am betting on no support from anyone else. I will most likely feel just like I did when my mom made me take stuff back by myself. She watched from a distance.

What I am advocating here is a culture of people who support each other in honoring the laws and good decency of the land. We need more patriots! We need more noble men and women who stand for honor and virtue and help others to do the same. We need great leaders who are willing to take a stand for the right. We need more people of courage to choose to do what is right, whatever the consequences might be. We need to help each other be good.

The world is shifting away from strong values and integrity. Many today think nothing of breaking the law a little bit here and there. Too many see no problem in cheating a little, fudging a little, lying a little, and otherwise distorting the truth and what is right—just a little. It is all too common to hear a news story about another group of people who cheated (and they are not all kids!), another person who violated common standards of decency, or someone who was unethical in some way. Every day, we see people willing to sell their integrity for the urgency of the moment. Sometimes, we seem to perceive that the only way we can get ahead is to manipulate the truth and what is right into something more palatable and definitely more competitive. The world's message may be "To get ahead, you do whatever it takes." And in this case, "whatever" truly seems to mean "whatever," even if the cost is a terrible one to bear.

What is the cost of all these breaches in integrity and honesty? What happens when we not only "break the law" but we encourage others to do the same? I don't know for sure what the global costs are. However, I can still feel the sting of regret for my dishonesty and for causing harm to others. I never seem to forget those events where I did not listen to conscience and acted in ways I ought not to have acted. If we multiplied just my youthful transgressions by how many people there are, we would have a significant amount of shame and guilt. Even if only a minority of people break the law, we are talking about a lot of people carrying regret for past bad choices.

Of course, in the climate of "everyone is doing it," we find an easy, conscience-numbing excuse not to listen to our inner voice telling us "No!" If we are all doing it, it is so much easier to hide in the weeds, not feel the weight of personal accountability and responsibility, and further justify wrong actions. This is not good. We will not feel any comfort when driving off a cliff if we look around and see everyone else plummeting too!

My mom gave me some good advice to help me with this. It may not change the entire world, but, perhaps, one person at a time, it will make a difference. Mom used to say:

"Jim, you have to live with yourself for the rest of your life. You don't have to live with me or anyone else. The only person you can never get away from is yourself."

Then, Mom challenged me to be honest and ethical, obeying the rules and laws of wherever I was. She encouraged me, saying that not only were these the right things to do, but I would have the peace of mind that always comes from doing what is right. She helped me to see I could at least feel good inside myself for the rest of my life. I have control of those feelings. By consistently choosing and doing what is right, I claim an abundance of assurance and confidence that regardless of outcomes, I will feel peace inside myself. This is a remarkable feeling. When absent because of poor choices, it is an empty feeling.

So let's all look deeply at ourselves, make a resolve to do what is right, and help each other to do the same. Let's help each other down the road with all the honesty and integrity we can muster. Then not only will we feel really great, but we will be really great!

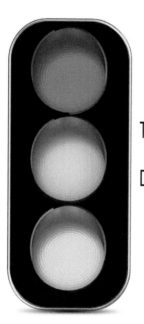

"THE BEST WAY TO GAIN STRENGTH WHEN HARD TIMES COME IS TO KEEP DOING ALL THE THINGS THAT MADE YOU AS STRONG AS YOU WERE TO BEGIN WITH."

Chapter 33

Stopping "I Brake for Tailgaters"

You can still see them on the backs of cars—bumper stickers that say, "I brake for tailgaters." To be honest, I have never really understood the point of this bumper sticker. What is the driver trying to say here? I think he's saying, "If you come too close to me, I am going to slam on my brakes and force you to crash into the back of my car." I cannot understand the logic of this—why would you want someone to rear-end you?

I have been hit a couple of times from behind. It was not a pleasant experience for me, and I hated all the headache (literal and figurative) that followed. My car was damaged. Police were called, tickets were issued, and months of repair work and inconvenience were in store for me. Also, it seemed my car was never quite the same after the accident. Once, my insurance premiums went up. Getting hit by a car is never a good experience. So why would I do anything that would make it *more* likely to happen to me?

As people, we are caught up in a similar pattern of behavior where we are willing to hurt ourselves to get back at someone we feel is hurting us. We have someone in our life doing something dangerous, hurtful, insensitive, and just plain wrong. I have counseled with hundreds of spouses of addicts, abuse and affair victims, and other people in situations where another person is causing harm to them. I have had to talk to the innocent party about this very principle so many times that it kind of scares me. Something in us causes us to do things that cause ourselves harm when someone is hurting us. People who were hurt by an affair will often seek to have an affair of their own to "even the balance." People married to addicts will often seek out addictions of their own. Even more common, people will stop doing all of the good things that help them to feel happy, confident, peaceful, and strong. Why do we do this? Most likely because we are in terrible pain and just want it to go away.

Let me be clear! Pain does not go away by doing something that will hurt or bring pain to you. Additionally, pain does not go away by stopping all activities that bring strength and confidence. It just does not work to "brake for tailgaters." I often tell people this behavior is like drinking poison and expecting someone else to die. When we are in the midst of hard times and challenging events, we need all the support and strength we can muster. Often, we casually say things like "Be grateful for your hard times; they make you stronger." Well, to be frank, this is only true if you make good and strengthening choices when trials come. To be sure, the best way to gain strength when hard times come is to keep doing all the things that made you as strong as you were to begin with. This is the real test of life—will you keep doing good things when the tribulations come? Will you stay on course, firmly entrenched in strong life patterns?

So when hard times come and you are tempted to hit the

brakes to get the person behind you to get off your back, remember these thoughts. If you are a praying person, keep praying. This is when you need God most! If you are a fitness buff, keep working out. This is a time where you will need all the health and strength you can muster. If you meditate, keep meditating. If you have close friends you normally spend time with, call them up, keep the usual routine of social events, and hold on to them. Whatever good you normally do, don't stop it because of the hurtful choices of another. Do what you know is going to keep you strong and feeling as capable as possible.

When someone tailgates me, I may slow down by letting up on the gas as appropriate. Usually this is because I want to increase the safe distance between me and the car in front of me. I don't want to be put in the situation of getting hit from behind and smashing into the car in front of me. Most often, however, I will find a quick way to pull over and let someone pass. I don't need to worry about that person hitting me from behind. I would rather have him racing off in front of me so I do not have to worry. I focus on my own safe skills and what makes the drive enjoyable for me. I will not let someone else's choices take that away from me. If you are innocent of wrongdoing, please do not suffer needlessly for others' bad choices. Stay on course! Do all the good things you need to do. Be assured you will find greater strength and resilience than you can possibly imagine by so doing.

Chapter 34

Eliminating Excuses

$\mathbf{I}$t seems every time my family heads down the road, the kids immediately get into a game of "Slug Bug." If you are a kid, have kids, or remember being a kid, you have probably played this game. Like me, you may have the bruises to prove it. My kids love to pound me and each other to win the game. In case you are not familiar with Slug Bug, it works like this: Whenever you see a Volkswagen Beetle, you call out, "Slug bug!" and then you punch the person closest to you. According to my kids, the punch needs to be hard enough to knock the person into the next zip code. When the person finally regains consciousness, it is essential to shout out "No slug backs!" This remark apparently has some sort of protective power forbidding the wounded one to strike back. For extra protection, you may also want to shout, "No pinch backs, bite backs, or ANYTHING backs!" This command provides you a limited shield until the other person sees the next Slug Bug first. Then, look out. If you slug and then forget to apply the protection, prepare to be bashed into a neighboring community. Never mind ejection seats; we just need Slug Bug!

One day, my wife became very frustrated with this activity. She was tired of the pounding and being pounded. She was tired of the wailing of the younger children: "Mommy, he shattered all my bones and crushed all my internal organs! I am going to die!" Then she heard the arguing. "I did not hit you that hard!" or "I only smacked you hard enough to knock off your braces! It was not that hard!" What was crazy fun had become calamity and chaos and no one was happy. In one of those frustrating moments, she blurted out, "We don't need an excuse to hit each other!"

Not missing a beat, the kids said, "OKAY!" and started punching each other. Another one of those great parenting moments. "Hooray!" they shouted. "We don't need an excuse to hit each other!" More pounding and crying, but now there is giggling and laughing at Mommy's little mishap. It is great no longer to need any excuses!

Of course, what my wife meant was that we should not hit each other at all—that we don't need an excuse to engage in harmful behavior to ourselves or others. I recommend applying this concept to your life. Don't make excuses for doing things that hurt you. Are you making excuses in any way for bad habits, not making changes you need to make, or not following through with something you ought to be doing? Are you excusing yourself because of a weakness, an illness, or some other real or imagined limitation? Is there anything keeping you from fully living your life to the fullest degree possible? If so, then maybe you need to stop making excuses! You don't need them anymore. Give them up!

Most of us know this already, or at least we have felt it: We are our own worst enemies when it comes to changing and improving our lives. It is so easy to let fear, procrastination, slothfulness, and even being too busy keep us from achieving all we can and want to achieve. It is just too easy to blame our health, our schedule, our work, our spouses, or the weather for not reaching our goals. I know! I have been there. It is so easy to do. It is so destructive to our innate wonderful potential. We need to stop making excuses and get moving.

So is it time for an honest look at all the things you are not achieving and the excuses keeping you from doing so? Start by taking an honest personal inventory of your life. Where are you falling short? Don't be afraid to take an inventory! I promise each of us has a list of things we can do to become better. The length of the list or the enormity of the challenges are not as important at this point. We all have them. There is great maturity in seeing that when it comes to progressing and growing, there is no such thing as "Done" or "I have arrived." It is like driving toward the horizon. Every time you get as far as you can see, there is more to see. We are never there! We are just constantly moving forward. So get that list going.

Then, after you have made a list, you can prioritize items in order of most needed to least needed to be done. It is often helpful to think of and even talk to others and get their input at this point. If you are willing to ask honestly for feedback, you will receive helpful guidance and instruction. Then, ask yourself the key question, "What excuses have I made to keep me from getting started on this goal or needed change?" You could write these all down. Again, you may ask your spouse or friend for some feedback. Be brave and say, "Will you please share with me what excuses you see me using for not making this change?" A true friend will tell you. A church leader or counselor may help with this as well. Support groups also are brilliant at helping with this.

Once you have this information, resist the temptation to get mad at yourself or feel bad. Making excuses has been a part of the human story from the very beginning. Adam ate of the forbidden fruit and said it was because of Eve. Eve made an excuse that the serpent gave it to her. I am sure the devil has some excuse for his behavior too! Resist the temptation to hide like they did and honestly look at your list and the feedback you received. Then, tell yourself, "I don't need any more excuses. I am going to get started today." If necessary to help yourself, you may also apply this mantra, "I don't have to do it perfectly. I don't even have to get it done right away! I just need to get started." All getting started requires is a fixed determination to live without any more excuses.

So stop pounding yourself about those things you have not been doing. Stop beating yourself up and not getting to the changes you really want to make in your life. Look yourself in the mirror and say to yourself, "I don't need any more excuses!" Then call out, "No Slug Backs!" and get moving! You will feel better and get some real momentum going.

Now if I just knew what to say when my kids see a PT Cruiser and yell "Cruiser Bruiser" and smack each other on the legs!

"DON'T BE SO ENGROSSED IN WHAT YOU ARE DOING AND WHERE YOU ARE GOING THAT YOU FAIL TO SEE THE IMPORTANT PEOPLE ALONG THE WAY."

Chapter 35

Clearing Off Your Windows

Many of you reading this book live in climates similar to Colorado. The winters can be harsh and driving is surely affected. When I was in high school, I had to park my car outside. I did not mind this in the pleasant Colorado summers, but I hated it when the frigid and snowy winters came. I especially hated cleaning off the ice and snow from my car. It would be my hunch most people also hate doing this. My evidence? Every winter I see cars covered in snow, sometimes with barely a five-inch circle cleared for the driver to see out. I have seen cars with literally three feet of snow on the hood and on the roof. The driver appears to have only thought enough to make a little spot of visibility. You can see him leaning all the way forward, face almost pressed to the frozen windshield, trying to see. I never do this! I clean off every inch of snow and ice I possibly can and will not drive until I can see clearly. And I have good reason for doing so.

I will never forget coming home from school one afternoon and having nothing to do. So I did something unusual for me; I sat down and read the newspaper on the table. I read a story that changed my life, and in a way, has haunted me since then. I can still remember the name of the boy in the story. His name was Hunter. He was two years old. Hunter was killed by a driver who could not see because his windows were covered with snow. The driver veered too far toward the sidewalk where poor Hunter was and killed him. I could not believe it. I felt horrified and resolved to take whatever time necessary to keep my windows clear. I never wanted something like that to happen because of me.

Are you driving with your windows covered? Are you so engrossed in what you are doing and where you are going that you fail to see the important people in your way? Too many times, we cut corners, tell ourselves it will be no big deal, and we casually race on. In life, it seems most of the time that nothing bad will happen. I can probably close my eyes for an extended period of time on those long and lonely highways through Nebraska and Kansas and not be harmed, but should I risk it? Most of the time, we make it okay. But what about that one time? If it happens one time, it can literally destroy you and others' lives forever.

I never met Hunter, but his story has stuck with me. Many years later, I met a young woman who, in one careless act, was responsible for the death of her best friend in a car accident. Many lives were forever altered that day. The girl was forever plagued with guilt and sorrow over what had happened. Close family relationships and friendships were destroyed. There were legal and financial consequences lasting for years. Many people were haunted for long after the accident. The consequences far outweighed the time it would have taken to be responsible. I was able to see both sides of the Hunter story now.

I know many stories of people harmed by what seemed, in the moment, to be innocent, fun, and harmless choices. I have been there to assist those who are devastated by a moment of carelessness. I have tried to offer some hope and comfort in those very trying and difficult moments. It is a hard place to be in. Some losses cannot be restored. Some choices cannot be changed. It is always better to clean the windows now and be as deliberate and careful as we can.

Chapter 36

Asking "Is It Me?"

While serving a two-year mission for my church in southern California, I had some incredible experiences, some difficult experiences, and some that helped shape how I have chosen to live my life. One of them was a very simple, yet impactful experience. We were headed to an appointment and arrived a few minutes before the scheduled time. We pulled up behind a small sports car with a license plate that read:

IZZITME

I have always been intrigued by so-called vanity plates and the ideas for them that people come up with. I like to figure out the complex ones and laugh about the silly ones. I tried for some time to solve this one, but I could not figure out what it meant. So, after our appointment, when our host was walking us back out to our car, I inquired about the meaning of this interesting plate. What he told me affected me in a profound way.

He told us he was an artist who was often hired to paint portraits. He described the arrangement of sitting directly in front of the person and sometimes taking hours to paint his or her portrait. He added, after a long time, the person almost always whined out this question, "Is it me?"

He told us in those moments, he never said what he wanted to say, something like "Oh, was I supposed to be painting you?" Or "Who did you think I was painting all this time and what did you think you were posing for?" He told us he would just smile and say, "Of course it is you!" And keep on painting.

For some reason, this whole experience really stuck with me. That night I was reading in the Bible about the Last Supper. Jesus reveals to his followers that he knows one of them will betray him. Then, it hit me. The Bible says the disciples all went around the table and asked, "Is it me?"

Putting the two together, I learned a valuable lesson for life—asking myself, "Is it me?" So if something goes wrong in my relationships, my work, a project I am overseeing, or other events, I ask myself, "Is it me?" I try to look for any evidence that would support me being the cause of or part of the problem. Often, especially with my children, I will just assume it is me and apologize.

Doing this has improved my relationships with my family members and my ethics and responsibility at work. When I die, I am not exactly sure what my kids will say about me, but I am pretty sure my kids will tell you I was always willing to apologize for my mistakes. Most people in my work setting know me as someone who works hard and does what he says he will do. This is in large part because I am asking myself, "Is it me?"

Great things can happen when we seek to take personal responsibility for the events and circumstances in our lives. Let's face it! It is quite easy to point fingers, place blame, and level accusations at other people. It is way too easy to find fault. However, when we start looking into the mirror instead of the magnifying glass, we see the truth. We, like everyone else we will ever meet, are not perfect. We make mistakes too! We have our own foibles and challenges to face each day. When we focus on ourselves and our roles, we reclaim the power to move forward. Asking, "Is it me?" helps make others feel better. Sometimes I apologize even when I know it is not my fault because it helps all of us to feel better.

Are you in the habit of blaming others, pointing fingers, or criticizing? Even more, are you feeling any burdens of guilt for things you have done wrong, corners you may have cut, or small lies you have told to cover your mistakes? If you are, there is no peace in this. You will never be happy blaming others or seeking to hide who you really are. True peace, lasting peace comes from personal responsibility and integrity. Asking, "Is it me?" is a great way to start obtaining that personal prize of peace. Start today. Take personal responsibility. Every so often, you will know it really is you. When you humbly see this, you can make changes. You can be better. See it for what it is. Take ownership. Then, get to work making changes for the better.

Chapter 37

Trash Truck Hits Cow During Rush Hour

This is not a joke! This was a very real traffic report I heard just prior to leaving to go home from work one day. I laughed out loud. How does something like this happen? I don't know what goes through your mind, but I have a lot of questions. I just cannot work this one out. What is a cow doing on the road? In rush hour traffic? You have to report this situation because it is too good *not* to report. I would bet the transportation department had nothing in its manuals for how to respond to this one. This is one of those events for which you cannot prepare. I am betting the first responders just figured it out as they went along.

Life is a lot like this. In spite of all of our efforts to plan, organize, and live a predictable life, some things happen for which we cannot prepare. Be they accidents, tragedies, losses, hurts, or other unplanned events, these things are often out of our control. No amount of efforts, structuring, or pre-posturing could have made it otherwise. Life has a way of handing us something to struggle with. What do we do in those moments? What do we do when nothing in life has prepared us for what hits us? What steps do you take when the Great iPad of Life has no answers or apps to work you through what just happened?

Well, I don't know everything, but you do what humans have always done at times like this—you keep going. You put one foot in front of the other and keep pushing on. You pray, you cry, you lose sleep, but you keep going. I have responded to many catastrophic, tragic, and even horrific events in my life. I have been a first responder after suicides, homicides, accidents, shootings, tornadoes, hurricanes, and more. I can tell you there is nothing you can do to prepare for some of these things. Yet I am convinced that if you take all you have and slowly and steadily move forward, the answers will come. You will make it through. You will be able to clean up the mess, solve the problem, hurdle the bar, and get back to safe driving.

So when life hands you the unexpected—when your cow gets hit by a trash truck during rush hour—laugh, lift up your chin, and face it. You can clear this up. The traffic jam will be over soon, and all rush hours eventually end. You can do this!

"IN THE RACE
TO FEEL
ADEQUATE AND
COMPETENT,
WE OFTEN FEEL
WANTING AND
LACKING IN
WHATEVER IT
IS THAT MAKES
SOMEONE
OKAY."

Chapter 38

Remembering You Are Okay

Whent so-called vanity plates came out, my mom decided to order a set for her car. Mind you, we were not rich or sophisticated in any way. To prove this, my mom drove a little red Chevy Chevette. My brother and I less than affectionately called it the "Chevy Shove-it!" It was basically a little pinball machine on wheels. Yet she still wanted to have her own personalized license plate. She cannot explain how she came upon the slogan for her car, but her name and anything close to her name was already taken. So she chose "I'm OK." When the plate arrived, we all were excited and it was placed on the back of the car. Then, as with all things like this, the excitement wore off.

Quite a long time later, we were driving down the highway when a car pulled up exactly parallel with us. The car matched our pace exactly and the driver began to honk to get our attention. When we looked over, the driver was holding up an obviously hurriedly scribbled sign that read "Says Who?" He then laughed and zoomed on. We were never able to answer him. Yet I thought of his question ever after.

We live in a world where people constantly question our

worth and value. We hear so often about the importance of good self-esteem, feeling good about yourself, and having strong self-confidence. We also hear almost daily of people who obviously did not like themselves, which led to challenges or problematic behavior for them. Even more, we are constantly looking around to see whether we are okay. We look to clothes, fashion magazines, movie stars, and celebrities as measuring sticks for our worth. Too often, we find ourselves lacking in something as we continually compare ourselves to someone or something else. In the race to feel adequate and competent, we often feel wanting and lacking in whatever it is that makes someone okay.

Something else happens in our ever-competitive world. We get messages like the one from our friendly partner on the road. When you express any kind of confidence or self-assurance, someone will always question you. One person will consider you egotistical and arrogant. Another will question your motives or wonder what you are hiding inside. Here is the irony. We want people to have positive self-regard, but when they do, we do something to question or cut them down. We constantly feel like we have to answer the "Says Who?" question.

Recently, my family bought me a T-shirt that reads "They told me I could become anything, so I became awesome." At first, I felt very uncomfortable wearing this shirt out of my home. Yet when I did, I received two responses. The most common response was people pointing at me and saying, "Love your shirt." The less common response was a person saying something similar to our driving friend's: "Says who?" When I noticed I was feeling uncomfortable wearing the shirt, I asked myself what was going on inside me. I am grateful I stopped to do this because I learned a valuable and helpful lesson about individual worth and self-confidence. I share it in hopes it will also help you.

I feel blessed to have had a mother who pushed me to achieve and do my best. I will be forever grateful she taught me to work hard and give my all. If I have achieved anything great in my life, it has roots in her confidence in me. However, I picked up a lesson along the way I don't think she intended to teach me. I know many others who have also unintentionally learned what I learned. Perhaps, you are one of those people. The message I somehow retained was that my worth and value was attached to what I did or what I became. In other words, my feelings of self-worth and self-love got attached to external markers of success. So good grades, praise, recognition, and achievement all became the indicators of my worth and value. For a while, this false belief can hold you. Yet the pleasure and satisfaction found in these markers of worth have a very short shelf-life. Their effectiveness is like a gallon of milk or bananas. They are nice and even give pleasure, but they are not going to be around for very long. A trophy, an award, and a medal are all really wonderful things. However, if you are not enough without them, you can never be enough with them. Worth has to come from somewhere else.

As I reflected on and prayed earnestly for answers regarding the "Says Who?" question, I learned a valuable truth. I did not have to become awesome. I already was awesome. I didn't have to earn worthiness or value. I came into the world as a possessor of these things the moment I arrived. There is no such thing as being okay or not okay. Worthiness is inherent in all of us. We don't have to acquire it. We cannot purchase it or even steal it. It already exists within all of us. The only acceptable answer to the "Says Who?" question might well be "Me!" Or perhaps the universe! Or God! It might even be "No one has to tell me I am okay! I just know I am. And so are you!"

I cannot fully explain what this realization did for me and my inner feelings. Now I am not rushing around seeking to get praise, recognition, or what I have come to call another stamp in my passport that says I have gone somewhere great. These things are nice, but I no longer need them. I am not as concerned about earning some kind of indicator that I am of worth or value. I am concerned about using my worth and value to make a difference in my world and the larger world. When I came to see I was worthy to begin with, it was easier to launch into all the things I have to do. I was no longer doing things to fill some cup full of holes. I was drinking from a well of worth, inner personal confidence, and a sense of self-assurance so nice to live with.

It is so much easier to head down the road not worrying about where my worth and value comes from. I have also stopped worrying about someone coming along to question my worth. I can drive on with an inner confidence drawn from my mother's license plates. "I'm OK" and so are you! Accept it! It just is true!

"ONE THOUGHT, CARELESSLY FLYING THROUGH THE MIND IN A VULNERABLE MOMENT, HAS THE POWER TO KNOCK YOU COMPLETELY OFF COURSE."

Chapter 39

Looking Out for the
Rear-View Mirror Effect

I felt cheated when I bought my first car. I know you are always taking a risk when you buy a used car from someone. I was tempted to call back the seller and give him a piece of my mind, but with a mind like mine, I needed all of the pieces I have! I did not have any recourse but to deal with it! I cannot believe he would not tell me my "new" car came with, not one, but two blind spots. Maybe you have purchased a car with blind spots. I am betting no one told you either! It is just unfair not to disclose this at selling time!

In spite of not knowing my car came with blind spots, I quickly learned to check them before I changed lanes. However, I came to learn there is an interesting and potentially dangerous thing that happens every time I check my blind spot. I found the very act of looking over my shoulder to check the spot caused me to start moving in that direction already. So while I am checking to see whether it is potentially safe to change lanes, I find myself already heading into the lane. This is not good if that lane is not clear! I have come to call this "the rear-view mirror effect." As soon as we start looking in a certain direction, we start moving in that direction.

The rear-view mirror effect can strike us in all aspects of our lives. Again, as soon as we start looking in a certain direction, without even intending to do so, we begin heading in that direction. In my work as a counselor, I see it the most in people who are feeling down on themselves. Secondly, I see it so often in those who are struggling with addictions. The rear-view mirror effect is part of why they are so self-critical or seemingly incapable of accomplishing their goals. It is so much a part of the pathway to addictions.

Here is how it might work and even happen for you. You are having a little bit of a rough day. Or you may even be having a horrendous day. In that moment, when you are all alone, frustrated, maybe scared, and feeling overwhelmed, you say something to yourself like "I just cannot do this!" Right here is where the rear-view mirror effect starts. The mind is so powerful! Literally, as soon as you say the words, "I just cannot do this!" you start moving in that direction. Your brain, almost as if it has a life of its own, takes you down a path of showing you every moment and every scene in your life where you had to wrestle with something. If you have given up or faltered in the past, I promise it will show up in your "blind spot." Then you will start to move, first in feeling and then in action, toward "I just cannot do this." You will feel more discouraged, more hopeless, and more burdened. Before you know it, your energy level will be depleted. You will be convinced inside that there is no point in continuing. If not checked, you may actually be unable (not because of lack of skill) to accomplish what you set out to do. You will be weakened in your resolve and sapped of your strengths. Simply put, you already moved from the "I can do this" lane to the "I just cannot do this" lane.

I see this all the time in people I work with. In the difficult, dark, and dreary moments of life, what we say to ourselves so often determines our direction. The inner dialogue or self-talk influences which way you go. It is more powerful than you can imagine. Never underestimate the power of thinking in these moments. One thought, carelessly flying through the mind in a vulnerable moment, has the power to knock you completely off course. So I regularly tell the people I am counseling to watch their thoughts because those thoughts are in fact moving them into one lane or another.

With addictions, it can be the same as what I just described. This rear-view mirror effect also is so much a part of the creation and maintaining of so many addictive patterns. Most people don't just sit down one day and say, "I think I would like to get hooked on drugs" or "I am going to start my computer gaming addiction today!" Often, the process is more subtle and almost smooth, kind of like moving from one lane to another. An addiction or the pathway to addictive acting out always begins with a small, seemingly insignificant statement in the head. In my work with so many addicts over the years, I have so clearly seen the rationalization, justification, minimizing, and objectifying that is happening. It is saying things like "I will just play for a few minutes!" or "It won't hurt to have just one drink! What difference does it make? I already screwed up," and so much more. These "little" looks move the person right into the lane of addiction. Once you look, you begin to move.

So what do you do if you struggle with self-concept and addiction? Well, as I already said, you start by watching your thoughts. You start to notice any thought that comes into your mind in these moments. Some people find it helpful to tune into any negative feelings or emotions that come and ask themselves, "What was I thinking right before I felt this way?" In this way, they can find those thoughts. Writing it down can make it even more powerful because it gets it out of your head and forces you actually to look at it—you are literally watching it as you write it down. Then, really examine the thought. Is it going to take you where you want to go? Many people I have worked with have asked themselves the following questions once they find the thought: "Is it true? Is it *really* true? Is there anyone in my life who would disagree with me about this? What is going on for me right now that I am thinking and feeling this way?"

Let me give you an example of how this process works. I was putting shelves in the garage. I had already drilled the holes for the shelves up 85 percent of the wall. Using the same measurements and process, I began to drill the next hole when water started spraying in my face. Shocked, I quickly raced to shut off the water and see what I had just done. Obviously, I had drilled through the plumbing. I was so discouraged and frustrated by this situation. I stood there in the garage feeling angry, incompetent, and foolish. Then I managed to stop myself. I decided to ask myself: What was I thinking right before I felt this way? I thought, "You are so stupid!" Quickly I saw the lane change. What came next was thoughts like "You should not be doing stuff like this! You are never good at things like this! You are too dumb to do this!" Then, I recalled all the times I had had mishaps or unfortunate things happen in the past, including some where it was clearly my fault. The lane change happened so fast that I was barely aware of it. In a matter of seconds, I went from feeling excited and confident about my shelves (I did have an 85 percent success rate so far) to feeling disturbed, downtrodden, and downcast. I went from secure and successful to stupid and incapable in seconds. Then, the tenderest of mercies, my son came out to see whether everything was okay. Without thinking, I said out loud, "I feel so stupid for drilling through the plumbing." In a sweet moment, he looked at me and spontaneously said, "Dad, you are not stupid. You could not have possibly known the plumbing was there." Immediately, I thought of the "Is it true?" questions above. He was right. I had no way of knowing. I felt immediately better. I was back in the right lane again. Sure enough, as I went to repair the plumbing, I could now see inside the wall and notice what I did not know before. It was clearly not stupidity. I just could not have possibly known. Regardless, with a little bit of looking at my thoughts and some compassionate words from my son, I was back on track.

If you are struggling with addiction, in a good moment, sit down with a piece of paper. Think about the last lapse you had into your addictive behavior. Ask yourself what thoughts you had well before you relapsed. What did you tell yourself? Root out any rationalizations or justifications. Then, take each of these statements and notice the lane change that happened. Go back and tell yourself the truth or the facts about each particular thought. If the thought was "I will just play one game" and you played for two hours, tell yourself the truth. It might look like "I never play just one game. It always leads to more." Do this with each of the thoughts you had before the slip. Enlist the help of a trusted friend, church leader, sponsor, or counselor if you need to do so. Find those little thoughts that led to the lane change.

We all have blind spots. When we look in the direction of the blind spot, the rear-view mirror effect kicks in. So often, if we are not alert and aware, we will begin to change lanes into a place we don't really want to be. Remember, the mind is powerful and the very act of looking causes you to move in that direction. So notice it. Watch for it! Be careful! Take whatever action necessary to keep from drifting and quickly get back into your safe lane. You can do this!

"AS LONG AS YOU KEEP MOVING FORWARD, PERSISTENTLY, YOU WILL ARRIVE."

Navigating Through the Parking Garage

Perhaps you have had the experience of having to find a parking space in a parking garage. If your experience was like mine, the garage was dark, cramped, crowded, and made up of lovely, stark gray concrete. You start at the bottom level and slowly work your way around. It is hard to see open spots, there is not much room to maneuver, and it feels as if you may never find a spot. You crawl slowly around each corner, cautious in the very narrow lanes, struggling to see clearly, and gradually moving upward. As you look around, you feel as if you will never find a spot and you wonder whether you will ever make it where you need to go. It can be very frustrating as you turn each revolution and see nothing but the same old concrete walls, the same cold, metal stairs, and the same dim flickering lights that remind you of a horror movie or a scene from *CSI*. Frustration sets in as nothing changes, no spots are available, and each turn looks just like the last. Then, you reach the top. You are almost blinded by the brilliant sunlight. So many spaces are available up here. As you pull in, you notice an incredible view made up of bright blue sky, billowy white clouds, and green trees and bright-colored flowers. Everything looks clear, clean, peaceful, and pristine. You have a quiet moment, soaking in the unlimited view in every direction. Spacious buildings, grand architecture, and grand vistas lie before you. You have arrived.

As I work with people struggling to overcome persistent problems, and they become discouraged, I find it helpful to describe the parking garage to them. It may feel like you are not making any progress. It may feel like it will be forever dark and scary. You may look around and tell yourself, "I am not making any progress at all because everything looks the same as the last turn I made." It seems that nothing at all is changing and you feel like you are most definitely not getting anywhere. Each turn just proves your inability to overcome and move forward. There seems to be no hope the light will ever come.

In those moments, remember the parking garage. It may actually look like you are not making any progress. Often, in seeking to surmount severe stresses, it takes several turns around similar corners to get there. Work is often required in the dark because we don't yet have all the answers, skills, or resources to make it any further. Yet be assured that if you keep going forward, rounding each curve, you will arrive. You may not be able to see it from your surroundings, but if you keep steadily on, you are climbing. You are rising with every forward step. When it seems like nothing has changed, when the bare concrete wall in front of you looks just like the last one, and when it feels like no forward progression has been realized, remember vividly the parking garage. As long as you keep moving forward, persistently, you will arrive.

Then, when you pull into the bright, morning sun, find all the spaces open, and a breathtaking spectacle before you, you will rejoice. You will have greater views of where you have come from, how far you really made it, and what you have learned. You will be able to see clearly what progress you really made, and feel better and stronger because of the climb. Life is a lot like the parking garage climb. The trick is to keep climbing and don't stop until you reach the top.

Chapter 41

Releasing the Brakes

I must confess, I have left the parking brake on too many times. It cannot be good for my car, but I do it often. You would think someone would make it impossible for this to happen, but it is possible. Many days, I back out of my driveway with the parking brake on. Then I shift to forward and try to move. The car seems sluggish, so I press on the gas harder. The car moves, but it feels like something is wrong. Then the realization hits me; I flat-forehead myself, and I release the brake. Suddenly, movement is so much easier and I am on my way. I could continue forward by pressing on the gas more, but it just works better when I release the parking brake. Life is a lot like this—especially when we want to change something.

We have all set New Year's Resolutions and other goals to make changes in our lives. It is natural to want to get better, look better, stop doing some bad thing, or improve upon some good thing. So we set a goal. In essence, we get in the car, start the engine, and step on the gas. Sometimes, some people race forward, heading right into the course of their objectives. They are successful. These people are not normal!

Most of us get behind the wheel of the car, step on the gas, and find the forward movement is difficult. We cannot seem to get things going. You see this a lot with diets and fitness goals. Maybe on January 1, it seems like this goal is achievable. We may sprint out of the chute, looking and feeling good. Then something happens and movement seems hard and sluggish. This can happen in the first ten minutes or in the first ten days. In fact, almost all of us hit up against this. What we were initially excited about and felt like we had momentum behind is suddenly dragging us down. It is hard to make progress. Discouraged, we may give up in these moments. We may even conclude it is not possible to change. Most of the time, we are wrong when we reach this conclusion. We just did not consider that the parking brake was probably still on.

When most people sit down to set goals, they focus on what they want to change, eliminate, achieve, or accomplish. This is good. It is best if we sit down and write these things down. If we can use proven formulas for getting good goals in place, even better. I personally like to use the SMARTS formula to set a good goal. A SMARTS goal needs to be **S**pecific, **Me**asurable, **A**ttainable, **R**ealistic, **T**ime-limited, and **S**tretching. If it does each of these things for you, it is a good goal. Writing it down makes it a great goal! If you share it with another person, it becomes a fantastic goal. Psychologist, author, and lecturer, Fitzhugh Dodson once said, "Goals that are not written down are just wishes." The same is true with a goal not shared with a loved one or trusted friend who can help and support you. Well-crafted goals, written down and shared with supportive others, are more achievable and produce better results. Then, you must track your progress. You can use a calendar, an app on your phone, or other methods. A worthwhile goal is one where you set it well, share it with others, and demonstrate accountability by reporting your results in writing. If you are not setting SMARTS goals, writing them down, tracking your progress, and sharing them with others, then I suggest you get started. A SMARTS goal might look something like: "I am going to exercise by running on my treadmill for thirty minutes per day, four to five times per week, for the next six months." It has all the elements of a successful goal.

This subject reminds me of an associate at work who asked me to ask him how his treadmill was every week. He shared with me his SMARTS goal and asked me to support him. So every Friday when we saw each other, I would say, "Hey! How is your treadmill?" He would usually respond with "It is great!" Occasionally, he would say, "A little dusty, a little dusty." I would respond with encouragement and a "You can do this!" and he went on his way. SMARTS goals with supportive tracking and supportive people are great!

However, we often miss a key part of goal setting, rarely mentioned in self-help books and counseling offices. It is found in the question posed by this chapter: Is your parking brake still on? In other words, when we set goals, we fail to consider the opposing or resisting forces or factors in our lives. We do not take the time to consider all of the potential obstacles that may prevent us from accomplishing our goals. Many of the goals we set are not achieved, not because they were bad goals, but because we failed to see and remove the obstacles to that goal prior to getting started. "Parking brakes" can take many shapes and forms. Sometimes they are found in negative people who make deflating and defeating comments like "You will never be able to achieve that!" or "I told you that you could not do it!" Parking brake people are the negative and even cruel people in our lives who keep us down. In my counseling work, I have seen hundreds of great goals ruined by these kinds of people. Other parking brakes may be health or financial concerns, time restraints, natural physical limitations, current habits, and unforeseen events. In summary, a parking brake is anything that keeps you from fully stepping on the gas toward your goal.

So sit down and set a SMARTS goal and put it into writing. Carefully devise a plan by which you will measure your progress. Then, share this goal with someone you love and trust, whom you know will not become a parking brake to you. Then, pull out another sheet of paper and ask yourself questions like: "What kinds of things might keep me from achieving this goal? What things could come up that may slow me down or make it harder for me to realize this objective?" I know some people who have to ask themselves, "What people in my life might sabotage my goal (such as bring you over a plate of brownies right after you start your diet) and keep me from achieving it?" You get the point! You are looking for any potential limitation, restriction, hurdle, obstacle, or impediment to your goal and its realization. Combined with your goal, your tracking plan, and your support person, you are now equipped to go forward.

So take the parking brake list and make a list to the right of it. You need to determine today, when setting the goal, what you will do to handle those obstacles. How will you release each of these parking brakes? Come up with a plan, what you will say to yourself, and how you will get through it. If helpful, ask your support person to help you in those moments. You could say something like: "I would like to ask for your support with my goal to exercise four to five times a week. I anticipate that I will have a hard time getting out of bed each morning. If I am not out of bed by 5:30 a.m., will you please come in and remind me of my goal?" Do you see how this works? You are still laser focused on your goal, and you are anticipating the parking brakes that will slow you down. It is so important both to set the goal *and* remove the obstacles. You need accelerating forces, and you need to remove any restraining forces.

Helpful hint: Some parking brakes are sneaky like mine on my little car. I did not even notice it was there. I did not anticipate that problem. So when you find yourself struggling with making progress toward your goal, look for a hidden brake. Most likely, there is one on and you need a plan to address it! Almost always, setbacks in goal achievement are related to unexpected obstacles or parking brakes. Find them, release them, and get back in gear and on the gas! Get moving as quickly as possible. Repeat as often as necessary.

Like my car with the parking brake on, we are also unable to move forward until we step on the gas and get in gear. However, we also must release the brakes. When we step on the gas and release the brake, watch out! We are moving now.

Chapter 42

Learning to Laugh Through Life

I have been blessed to have family members who have known how to make the most out of life. I am grateful for those who have taught me how to laugh at myself and many of the things that happen each day. It is good to know how to laugh at yourself and your mistakes. We all make them. Instead of getting upset, we can laugh it off. Two stories come to my mind when I think of those who taught me this lesson.

First, my great-aunt was a complete crack-up! She had so much fun that it almost felt wrong. She knew how to laugh and enjoy her life. This story illustrates how well she made this happen. Aunt Frannie went to the hairdresser almost every week. It was important to her. So in her usual routine, she had her hair perfectly dressed and headed out for her day. She decided to stop at the carwash. She pulled up to the console and entered the payment information. Then she pulled into the carwash. She had failed to roll up the window, and as soon as her car hit the right spot, the water started to spray. It came so fast that she could only panic. With a full spray of soapy water coming at her, she tried and tried to get the window closed. Screaming and flustered, she could not make it happen. At the end of the wash, she looked at herself in the mirror. On her right, her hair was perfectly coiffed, just as she loved it. On the left, her hair was matted, dripping, and soapy. That side looked awful. So she decided to go back to the hairdresser. Aunt Frannie tried to sneak in and quietly approach the front desk. Just like in the movies, as she approached, she was noticed, and in a shockingly loud voice, the attendant said, "Frannie! What happened to you?" Motioning for him to come closer, and whispering so as not to draw any more attention to herself, she whispered, "I just went through the carwash with my window down." Shocked, he shouted, "YOU WENT THROUGH THE CARWASH WITH THE WINDOW DOWN?!" Now, everyone was looking. Here she was looking like a half-abused Cruella De Vil with everyone staring at her. What else could she do but laugh? And get her hair fixed. I think she hoped for a half-off sale that day!

The second story is from my grandmother. Grandma loved the shopping catalogues that arrived in the mail. Most of us consider these catalogues full of junk, but she loved them and spent a ton of money on these things. (I am so grateful she lived before shopping channels!) Once she saw an ad for a rear-view mirror for the car that boasted "Now a mirror where you can *really* see everything!" So she ordered it. It was about three feet long and had all kinds of little mirrors on it. She was excited about it and went to place it in her car. She removed the old mirror and used the included double-stick tape to put up the mirror. For some time, she used it and bragged about it. She loved her see-all mirror!

Then one very hot summer day, the mirror fell off the windshield and on to the front seat. You guessed it; the mirror was sticky-side up. She sat on the mirror and did not realize it. So she went on her way, not noticing the mirror's absence. She arrived at the store and went in to do her shopping. While bending over, she felt a tap on her shoulder. A very nervous woman stuttered to her while pointing at Grandma's back-side, "Excuse me, ma'am, but you have...um...ah...um...."

Without missing a beat, Grandma reached back, yanked the mirror off her bottom, and stated assertively, "That is my rear-view mirror!" Then she quickly moved on!

My family and I have laughed about these two stories (and more) over the years. They have become our examples of how to handle the frustrating experiences of life. We have tried to follow Grandma and Aunt Frannie's examples and laugh at ourselves, laugh at the funny things that happen, and find joy in the unfortunate and wacky stuff that happens so often. When I dropped a whole container of salsa on the floor and it splattered all over the ceiling, my head, my shirt, and my tie, I looked at the terrified faces of my kids as they feared an angry dad. In that moment, I remembered what my grand-mother and aunt had done and followed their lead. What came next was a funny experience and another family story to teach this example. I asked, "Does anyone have a chip?"

So learn to laugh at yourself. Find ways to laugh about life. Add more fun to each of your days by laughing about all the crazy things that happen. Heck, you can even laugh at the boring, monotonous, and awkward things that happen. Then, don't stop there. Tell someone else! Don't just whisper it! Tell someone else what happened. Let them laugh at you and with you. Spread the funny stories and spread the laugh-ter. It makes this life so much better when we do!

Chapter 43

Stop Playing "Jerk"

Imagine a cozy Saturday afternoon, lounging in your favorite chair, reading a book and drinking lemonade. Unexpectedly, you hear the joyful playing of your children, ages four, three, and two. They are laughing and having a wonderful time. Every parent needs a moment like this, just basking in the greatest joys of life—a comfortable home, a beautiful day, and the most wondrous sounds of children coming from the other room. This is heaven on earth. You sit back, not reading anymore, so you can just listen to your playful and energetic children. Ah, to be a child again. In pure delight, you listen more intently to their conversation:

"Let's go play Jerk!"

"Yeah! I love that game! I get to be the Jerk!"

"NO WAY! You always get to be the Jerk! It is my turn to be the Jerk first!"

"NO ME! ME want to be Jerk! ME be Jerk first!"

Well, your peaceful reverie has ended. You are not familiar with this game and you are not sure it sounds very wholesome. Even more, you cannot imagine what this game will entail and you become concerned. So wanting to see it through, you sneak closer to find out what is going on and what your children are doing. Before you can get to them, you hear the slam of the back door and your kids heading outside. You creep to the window, not wanting them to hear you, thus interrupting this curious activity. When you get to the window, you get the surprise of your life.

All three of your children are on their tricycles and bikes. They are riding around on your large patio. They have quickly set up makeshift traffic lanes. Two of the kids are lined up at what appears to be an intersection. The other child has moved farther away. When the call to begin comes, the two younger children pull slowly forward on their way. Then the oldest comes racing around the corner, swerving right in front of his younger siblings. In feigned shock, they swerve their little vehicles in different directions, and you suddenly realize how this game got its name. The younger children shake their hands in the air and shout, "YOU JERK! YOU JERK!"

The kids laugh and get back together to decide who gets to be the next Jerk. You watch for a few more uncomfortable seconds before you detach yourself from the scene. You no longer feel peaceful inside, and a tinge of shame and guilt creeps over you. You recognize the scene and know exactly whom your children were imitating. You can see in your mind's eye, not just one scene, but many, where you did just what they were playacting. No parent of the year award this year for you!

This happened to my mother many, many years ago. In that powerful moment, she had the stark realization that she was being observed and imitated by her children in everything she did. Truth be told, we *all* are. Every moment of every day, someone is watching what we do. In every choice we make, we are teaching someone about that choice. For good or bad, someone is watching what you do, listening to what you say, and may just be following your example. This is especially true if you have children, grandchildren, or are regularly around children. You are a model of what to do. You may not have chosen to be such, but nevertheless, you are. People are watching. Do you want them to copy you?

Admirably, my mother decided to change the way she handled the people who frustrated or disappointed her. What will you do when faced with the expected frustrations and disappointments that surely will come to you? Will you react in a positive way, one someone could copy to your pleasure? Or will you feel a touch of shame or regret at having taught something you would never wish repeated (and definitely would not want traced back to you)?

I once volunteered to teach my church's before-school religion classes, called seminary. There were about six of us teaching a large group of high school students every weekday morning at about 6 a.m. One morning before class was to start, one of the teachers shared an experience illustrating the importance of watching how you conduct yourself. She had just taught a lesson to her seminary students about not smoking. Later in the same day, she was getting gas for her car. Unconsciously, she took her little white pen and put it in her mouth, holding it between her lips so her hands could be free while she filled up the car. Unknown to her, one of her students was across the parking lot. What do you think the student thought she was seeing? Fortunately, the teacher later learned what this student perceived. She talked of how important it was to be a good example because you never know who is watching.

I find this possibility motivating. Often, I will think about who might be watching. As a father, I am guessing my children are not only watching, but recording every action I take for good or evil. Sometimes I think they are looking for evidence against me to use at some later date. Occasionally, I receive quiet thanks from them when they comment on something they saw me do. Most often, they say nothing. It is hard to be the example I need to be all the time, but I find it easier if I remember who might be watching me. I never want someone to falter or struggle because of something he or she saw me do or not do. I am striving to be true wherever I go. I want to walk a little plainer so I won't have to worry about who may be following me.

Occasionally, I also think of those who will descend from me through my children and their children. I wonder what they will think of me and my choices. Will they be happy with what I did? Will they be proud to carry my name? Will they be grateful for the legacy I left them? Even they may be watching or looking back to me some day. I want them to be proud of who I strived to become.

So please take a moment and think about all those who may just be following you and what you do. Think about your family, your neighbors, your friends, your coworkers, and others. Who might be watching what you do and say? Among those people, is there anyone "playing Jerk" because of what he or she saw in you? If the answer might be "Yes," take action today to change what you are doing. You will feel good about it. You will feel stronger because you made a change to affect another in a positive way. It will make an impact. Teach what you really want to teach in both word and deed.

"EVERY MOMENT OF EVERY DAY, SOMEONE IS WATCHING WHAT WE DO. IN EVERY CHOICE WE MAKE, WE ARE TEACHING SOMEONE ABOUT THAT CHOICE."

Chapter 44

Leading So Others Can Follow

My father was always really into having a nice car. So, about every couple of years, he would get a new one. Often, it was something pretty sporty and very fast. My personal favorite was the souped-up, fully-loaded Trans-Am with a racing engine in it. It was incredible! I loved it when my dad let me drive his car. He let me take it to prom one year! The roar of the engine, the feel of your body being pressed against the seat as you accelerated—it felt wonderful. It was an incredibly fast car! I loved that car!

I also hated that car! I had a love-hate relationship with this car because whenever I had to follow my dad somewhere, it turned out to be a nightmare. My dad would say, "Just follow me." Then he would hop behind the wheel of this super-charged car and race off. Meanwhile, I was still trying to get to 20 mph in my 1970s silver, Pinto station wagon. I would barely look up and he was already gone. This happened every time he asked me to follow him somewhere. He raced off and left me literally in the dust. He could whip in and out of lanes, race through yellow lights, and speed off. My car just did not work that way. I remember getting lost many times because of my dad and his car. It was never a good experience. Often, he did not even use a turn signal. He would just race off with seemingly no thought for me and what I needed so

I could follow him. I learned a lot from these experiences about leadership and helping people to follow you. I have needed those lessons. I'd like to share some of them with you.

First, I learned to think more about who was following me than about myself and what my car could do. Because I had "been there," I knew how it felt to be left behind, lost, and unsure where to go next. I remember feeling inadequate as my little car could just not keep up. So when I became the leader, I first tried to put myself in the shoes (or in the car) of the person following me. I cared enough to want that person to feel as if he or she were going to be able to follow me. At this point, I have not communicated anything to the person. It is all an internal decision for me. I want to be the kind of person someone can follow. So I will take the time to make sure you feel you can follow me. This may include taking more time, listening more, and being willing to slow down. The primary mechanism for me is seeking to be empathetic. I try to remember and imagine what it was like for me all the times I had to follow someone when I did not know where we were going. Then I work to do all I can to prevent that feeling in those who come behind me. So my behavior will change as I do this. Metaphorically speaking, I am going to drive slower, be more deliberate, and provide more instruction and encouragement. I want people to know I understand them.

Second, I focus on anticipation more. In this case, anticipation means seeking to look down the road at all the person might need to know or experience to feel safe in moving forward. This may mean I am going to give verbal instructions, describing each step along the way. If necessary and helpful to the follower, I may also take the time to write out the directions or draw a map. I will take the time to anticipate what this person needs and provide it. He or she may walk away with a verbal description to have a vision of where we are going and directions and a map to get there. I have found it incredibly helpful and calming to followers when I take the time to do this well before the time to follow. When I care enough to anticipate their needs before we even get on the road, it creates confidence in my followers. They know I care about them because I took the extra time to anticipate what it might be like for them and what they need.

Third, I find it is essential to focus on the relationship. This means I need to listen very well. I will take the time to get to know someone first. So I am going to ask about the person's family, interests, likes and dislikes, and more. I am going to look for strengths. I am going to look at what resources the person has. I am going to look for resilience and how well he handles stress and pressure. I am also going to look for any indicators of opportunities to get stronger. I want to know where this individual might need more support and help. In short, I want to know how comfortable she is "behind the wheel." Knowing what he or she brings to the situation helps me so much.

Fourth, I am going to seek to be a model rather than a critic. I am going to try to show people rather than just tell them. I strive to follow the motto of never asking people who follow me to do something I have not or am not willing to do. I have even done this with my counseling strategies. I am not likely to recommend an approach I have not been willing to do myself. I am going to seek to be an example of whatever the tasks are. I am not just going to tell; I am going to show. In almost all of my jobs, I have been a trainer of some sort or another.

Often, I would say, "I am going to show you how to do the job. Then I want you to do it just the way I did it. I won't expect you to do it just the way I did it, but I want to make sure you know what the job is and how to do it. Then, once you have mastered it, you can adjust the process any way you like." In this way, people know that I know how to do the job and can demonstrate it with confidence to them, knowing they will have the latitude to do it "their way" in the future.

Finally, I seek to be an encourager. I want them to feel my confidence in them and my belief that they can do it! I have benefitted from people who expressed and showed trust and faith in me. I want to show this to those I lead. So I offer a lot of praise and gratitude. In the early stages, this may even seem like it is too much, but I find people love it. Everyone loves to be sincerely told he or she is doing well. So in the early stages, people get a lot of graciousness and cheerleading. I want to recognize any positive effort to change. It is easier to learn and grow when you know someone else believes in you.

Like me, you have been in situations where you did not know where you were going and what it took to get there. Will you remember how this felt and act accordingly when you are going to take the lead? Will you have empathy, anticipate the needs of your followers, and be a listener, an example, and a true support?

When my dad was leading the way, I so desperately wanted to follow him. I wanted him to drive slowly enough for me to follow him. I wanted him to understand I had the desire to go as fast as he did, but I was not able to yet. I wanted him to think of me before he changed lanes and to help me know, well in advance, where we were going. I was already impressed with what he could do in his car, but I wanted to know he was thinking more about me and what I might need as I followed him. I wished for him to understand my nervousness, inexperience, and even fear when he took us out on the road. I felt it would be helpful to know he was more interested in me than in getting wherever we were going.

Aren't we all like this? We need leaders who will truly lead so people can follow. You can be a great leader for others!

Chapter 45

Getting Started

I love driving a car with a manual transmission or a "stick shift." I like the feeling of control I experience as I regulate the speed, the RPMs, and when to shift. I love being able to manage the snow-covered roads, slick spots, and other road conditions using the gears. I am grateful I learned to drive a stick shift. Almost all of my cars have had a manual transmission.

I have not always felt this way. I hated my car when I was first learning to drive. It was an absolute nightmare. If you learned to drive a stick shift, you know what I am talking about. The whole process of having to push on the gas pedal just the right amount while lifting the clutch with the other foot just the right amount was terrifying. If you did it wrong, you either squealed the tires, or more likely, killed the engine. Sometimes, you jerked and stuttered your way forward, desperately trying to get the right balance between the left and right feet. It was so difficult! I also struggled with moving the lever at the wrong moment, resulting in a teeth-rattling, grinding sound. It hurt your hand as you realized you were not in gear. I was trying to balance the pedals *and* get the gear shift in the correct place. For me, it was almost too much to handle. It seemed it should be easier. Fortunately for me, I had no other option, so I stuck with it. I learned quickly that getting started and going was the absolutely hardest part. Going from no movement to forward movement took some time, patience, and practice. Then, once there was enough momentum, the other gears were easier. The faster I was going, the easier it was to manage. Getting started was the hardest part.

Life is a lot like this. Anytime we are desirous to change something in our life, the hardest part is always getting started. If you are at all like me, you usually have an idea of something you want to change. You may feel excited about it, or it may be something you just know you have to change. So you start to develop the desire to make the change. Finally, the time for action has come, and in some fashion or another, you start going. At first, there is enough excitement that it does not seem as difficult. Yet when the novelty wears off, the reality of the challenge kicks in. That is when it is difficult to manage the struggle to change. Now it is hard.

I found when learning to drive a car that it helped to focus on the clear objective. At first, it was just to learn how to drive confidently and safely. Second, it was actually to get some place. In order to accomplish these objectives, I had to get started. This meant I had to accept some "hits" at the front end before I would get going. I had to deal with the stutters, stops, halts, jerking, and tire squealing that came. I also had to deal with all different kinds of terrain, different traffic circumstances, and my own and others' expectations. It was a lot.

When we seek to change something in our lives, it is important to remember it will be just like driving a car with a manual transmission. It will involve all of the same elements. It will be exciting at first. It will be frustrating as you get farther along. You will kill the engine. You will burn off some rubber. You will get a mild whiplash as your car jerks back and forth until you get the gas and clutch just right. These are just reality. Then, you have to do it again at the stop sign, at the traffic light, when your friends are watching, and on slopes and hills of all sorts. Just when you think you are getting it, something else will come up that you will have to address. Yet if you keep your eyes on the goal of driving, admit it will be hard getting started, and practice just enough, you will succeed.

Too many people quit at the first sign of difficulty. We decide to diet, but we quit the first time we overeat or cheat. We decide to exercise, but we stop as soon as our muscles become sore. We decide on a new approach to parent our kids, but we stop as soon as the kids rebel or don't exactly respond. We quit before we ever get going. We never get the momentum behind us, so we don't experience the change and growth we wish to have.

Think with me on this for a minute. Imagine I get behind the wheel of my car, with the manual transmission. I have never driven a car before, but I passed the test, I have my permit, and I am so excited to get going. However, I have determined inside that if I cannot get going this very first time, I am not going to drive ever again. What do you think of this? You might be saying, "Better get a bus pass, pal!" How many days would you expect me to be driving if I had this goal? You called it! I would have quit on the first day! Truthfully, I would have quit after the very first time. Yet, let's pretend I did not mess up the very first time. I still would not have made it past the first day. It was hard. Even if I had given myself the so-called magic twenty-one days necessary to get good at something, if I quit the first time I messed up,

I would not have made it to day twenty-two. All change, all movement, all new directions are difficult to start.

So I came to expect those hard moments. I knew I was going to struggle and kill the engine or squeal out! It was just the way it was. The same is true with anything else I have started. I expect it to be hard. The muscles are going to hurt, the craving will be strong, the kids will rebel, and the habit will be hard to entrench. So I anticipate the difficulties. It always gets harder before it becomes easier. It is even harder before it becomes natural. If I am going to get from dead stop to racing down the road in anything, I am going to have to go from "I don't have any idea how to do this" to "I don't think I can do this!" to "This is really hard!" to "I am starting to get it!" to "I am awesome and I think I have it down!"

So look for the hard times to come. Look for the challenge. Look for the push back, the resistance, and the difficulty. In those moments, don't you dare quit! Don't you dare even think of stopping or setting it aside! Stay at it. Keep working. Make minor adjustments as needed, but don't you quit! Hang in there.

A Final Note: Let's Get Going

By now, you have learned a lot about life and how to make it better, and you have thought of things you could do. In some ways, you are already acting on the things you heard and learned. Most likely, you have been driving and you had one of these "driving lessons" come to mind and you did something differently. Maybe it was earlier today when you let someone in as he merged into your lane instead of speeding up like you usually do. Perhaps you stopped and got some lemonade from a young child, or you noticed something you had not seen before in yourself as you headed down the road. These are great things!

The first step to any change is to notice what needs to change. It is kind of like that feeling of needing to get out of the house and go somewhere. Now that you have that feeling, it is time to get behind the wheel and get moving. In fact, since you made it to this point in the book, you are already on the road. What you do next on this trip is up to you now! I challenge you to make it a good trip. Take a moment and reflect on what you have learned. If it works for you, jot down some key lessons, notes about a goal you want to achieve, or the name of somebody you want to contact to improve a relationship. Then, you must act. You must now drive to the places and things you want most in life. Take these driving lessons and make them work for you by doing the work. Your life is no longer driving you. You are in the driver's seat. Let's get going!

In this book, you learned about getting started toward living life more safely and happily. You learned more about your emotions and how to make the most of them. You learned to control "road rage," laugh at yourself, and make better decisions. You learned to persist in your goals by stepping more on the gas. You also learned to release the brakes. You know not to make excuses anymore, and so much more. Hopefully, you have had a fun time doing it, too! Take all the energy and enthusiasm you have now and let's get going!

Now it is time to hit the road. You are ready to graduate from "driving school." Imagine me handing you the keys, shaking your hand, patting you on the back, and pointing you down the road. I have confidence in you! You can do this! Let's get going!

If at any point you want a refresher, come back to these pages and review them again and again. Remember, these lessons will come to mind when you drive. Decide each time one comes to mind to act differently and make a change. Actually do it. Turn on your blinker, make the lane change, hit the gas, and get moving. You are ready! Let's get going!

I would welcome the opportunity to hear from you! To make comments about this book, tell me about your own driving lesson experiences, or to get more assistance, please contact me. I would be more than happy to have a complimentary, no-cost, consultation call with you. I promise you I won't show up with a clipboard and pencil! Just you and me and another driving lesson. I can best be reached at drivinglessonsforlife@gmail.com or at my website www.drivinglessonsforlife.com. Please contact me.

Let's get going!

About the Author

Jim R. Jacobs is an author, professional speaker, counselor, life coach, and entrepreneur. As a licensed clinical social worker (LCSW), he enjoys the opportunity to assist individuals, couples, families, and regional ecclesiastical leaders with social and emotional challenges. Jim specializes in treating those with depression, anxiety, obsessive compulsive disorder, PTSD, sexual addictions, and marital and family issues. He has always loved the opportunity to provide counseling and feels he has found his dream job.

Jim loves his family more than anything and treasures the experience of being a father. He is also active in the local community, including recently playing his alto saxophone in a local community band. Additionally, he is the treasurer for the city cultural council, seeking to bring the arts more fully into his neighborhood and community. He is devout and active in his local church and regularly volunteers his time as a leader, teacher, and more.

Jim graduated with a Bachelor's degree in Psychology from the University of Northern Colorado. After his graduation, he was immediately hired to coordinate programs for the disabled and traumatically brain injured in the Denver Metro Area. He also had opportunities to direct social service programs for poor and needy children, the elderly, and other vulnerable populations. In relentless pursuit of his dream to help others, he set aside a great career to pursue graduate studies at Brigham Young University. Jim graduated with a Master's degree in Social Work (MSW) and was recruited by LDS Family Services where he has worked for the past fifteen years. His work has taken him across parts of the nation, working in Utah, Nevada, Florida, and Colorado. Most recently, he has had the pleasure of overseeing the work of all agency operations in the largest area of the central United States. This has given him the opportunity to work and train others in many locations, including Chicago, Minneapolis, Kansas City, Helena, St. Louis, and Omaha. He loves his work and the people he works with. He considers his associates to be his greatest friends and supporters.

Jim is an avid reader who has loved self-improvement books since an unknown benefactor saw something in a fifteen-year-old server at the local pancake house and gave him a couple of large boxes of books. He is forever grateful she expressed belief in this unknown kid and inspired him with great works on self-improvement, management, leadership, and personal growth. Jim also enjoys reading inspirational books, fiction, and just about anything. Jim loves genealogy research, playing his alto saxophone, refinishing old furniture, and the sport of fencing. He has dreamed about writing this book and the one to follow for a long time!

You can learn more about **Jim R. Jacobs** via his website www.drivinglessonsforlife.com or on his Facebook page Driving Lessons for Life. For a free personal consultation or to engage Jim in a speaking opportunity, please feel free to contact him at drivinglessonsforlife@gmail.com.

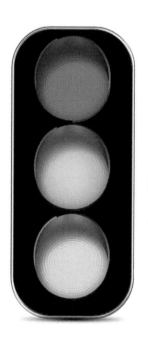

"ALL
GETTING
STARTED
REQUIRES IS
A FIXED
DETERMINATION
TO LIVE
WITHOUT ANY
MORE
EXCUSES."

About Driving Lessons for Life:

Consulting and Coaching

Jim R. Jacobs, LCSW has over twenty years of experience consulting, counseling, and coaching others to success. Trained in psychology and social work, Jim has the special training to understand both the personal and social dynamics that contribute to success. He has the unique ability to assess strengths, talents, and opportunities on the individual level and then move to assessing the larger social environment to determine what supports and obstacles exist. Jim uses a positive, strength-based method to combine the individual assets with social support to help achieve progress and success. He is skilled at helping individuals, families, groups, and leaders remove challenges and realize their dreams and destinies. Jim is positive, optimistic, enthusiastic, and passionate about helping people grow, realize their potential, and have the most happiness and success possible.

Please contact Jim R. Jacobs today for a complimentary, no obligation, consultation on your goals and desires. Let Jim help you to be all you can be and get where you want to go in life! Connect with Jim online at www.drivinglessonsforlife.com or by e-mail at drivinglessonsforlife@gmail.com.

Book Jim R. Jacobs
to Speak at Your Next Event

When it comes to choosing a speaker for your next event, you will find Jim R. Jacobs to be an engaging and enthusiastic presenter. Jim is likeable, dynamic, sensitive, and powerful in reaching his audiences. He can engage a small group or enthrall a very large crowd. Jim has delivered hundreds of trainings to audiences large and small in numerous states. He can easily adapt to meet your needs.

Over the past fifteen years, Jim has been especially sought out for women's conferences, seminars for adults, devotionals, and leadership training meetings. He has spoken on diverse topics, including overcoming depression, conquering addiction, strengthening marriage and family, supporting loved ones with addictions, and more. He is well-known as a trainer for ecclesiastical leaders who are seeking to improve their effectiveness as they minister to their congregation's needs. Additionally, Jim has been a dynamic trainer for individuals who desire to teach strengthening marriage and family classes. He has a passion for helping individuals, couples, families, and ecclesiastical leaders.

Jim also has experience speaking and training in a variety of settings. He has trained in outdoor arenas, hotel conference rooms, church buildings, webinars, teleconferences, studios, and via satellite broadcast. He has spoken to groups as few as 10 people and as large as over 5,000.

Jim offers a dynamic mix of stories, spirituality, humor, challenges, and inspiration according to the group's needs. He will take the time to meet with leaders and organizers to learn the desired goals and outcomes of the meeting and present to those needs. He thrives on creating a presentation that is memorable and practical. He enjoys being in front of the large group, but he will be found after the meeting seeking to mingle with and offer encouragement to the individual. He will leave people with meaningful information and magnifying inspiration. Book Jim R. Jacobs today!

To determine whether Jim is right for your event, please feel free to visit his website www.drivinglessonsforlife.com or e-mail him at drivinglessonsforlife@gmail.com.

Just Keep Driving

When I was sixteen years old and driving my very first car, I had a terrifying experience with a giant puddle of water. Or rather, I thought it was a puddle. I was heading to an appointment and missed my turn. So I quickly turned into a large parking lot to turn around and get back to my destination. It had been raining, so it was not odd to me to have the empty parking lot covered with what looked like a thin layer of water. So in my rush to get to my meeting, I drove right into it. Imagine my horror as I quickly came to know that this was not just a little bit of water on a flat parking lot. It is almost impossible in some circumstances to judge the depth of water, but I could tell by the sudden vertical descent of my car that I had just driven into a very large hole. I thought I might discover the truth behind the old movie *Journey to the Center of the Earth* because it felt like I was heading there. I was terrified!

Fortunately for me, I was a new and inexperienced driver with no idea how to handle a situation like this. So I did the only thing I could think of in that moment. I slammed the accelerator down. A giant wave of water washed over the car, but my action propelled me upward and right out of the puddle. If you showed me an instant replay, I would not have been surprised to see a large hand lifting me out of the puddle. It felt almost magical and miraculous how quickly I lifted out of the hole. On the other side, I felt my heart racing with the adrenalin rush. Yet it appeared I was completely unharmed and my car was fine after its sudden baptism by complete immersion. So I did what any sixteen year old would do—I drove on.

Life is often like this. We cannot possibly know everything about the journey in front of us. There will be obstacles in front of us we could not possibly imagine and for which we could not possibly prepare. There will likely be unseen pits masked by cool calm waters we could find ourselves falling into as we travel on. However, we may take courage in my response. Keep going. Step on the gas. Take the challenge head-on with all of your strength and energy. Sometimes you just need to plow forward with all your might to make it through. There may be times to stop and strengthen, but many problems are best handled by pushing on and pushing through to the other side. When life hands you such an unexpected challenge, push on through it!